Selling
a New World

Selling a New World:

Two Colonial South Carolina Promotional Pamphlets

BY THOMAS NAIRNE AND JOHN NORRIS

Edited with an Introduction by
Jack P. Greene

UNIVERSITY OF SOUTH CAROLINA PRESS

Copyright © University of South Carolina 1989

Published in Columbia, South Carolina, by the
University of South Carolina Press
First Edition

Manufactured in the United States of America

Library of Congress Cataloging-in-Publication Data

Selling a New World : two Colonial South Carolina promotional
   pamphlets / by Thomas Nairne and John Norris ; edited with an
   introduction by Jack P. Greene.—1st ed.
         p. cm.
      Includes bibliographies and index.
      Contents: A letter from South Carolina / Thomas Nairne—
   Profitable advice for rich and poor / John Norris.
      ISBN 0-87249-608-2
      1. South Carolina—Economic conditions.   2. South Carolina—Social
conditions.   3. South Carolina—History—Colonial period, ca.
1600–1775—Sources.   I. Nairne, Thomas, d. 1715. Letter from South
Carolina.   1988.   II. Norris, John. Profitable advice for rich and
poor.   1988.   III. Greene, Jack P.
HC107.S7S45 1988
330.9757′02—dc19

88-26108
CIP

Contents

Preface

This book reprints with annotations and an introduction two of the most informative promotional pamphlets published during the colonial period: Thomas Nairne, *A Letter from South Carolina* (London, 1710), and John Norris, *Profitable Advice for Rich and Poor* (London, 1712). Reissued in London in a second edition in 1718 and a third in 1732, the Nairne tract was republished except for one paragraph in the mid-nineteenth century in the *University of North Carolina Magazine, IV,* no. 7 (September 1855), 289–305, while a few short segments of the Norris work were included in H. Roy Merrens, ed., *Colonial South Carolina Scene, 1697–1774* (Columbia, 1977), 38–55. But this volume is the first republication in full of either pamphlet since the eighteenth century. It is here offered to readers in the hope that, like the editor, they will find it revealing both of conditions in early colonial South Carolina and of the nature of the appeals used to persuade people to immigrate to the colonies.

Of the two, the Nairne pamphlet is much less rare. In the United States, copies of the first edition may be found in a number of libraries, including the Library of Congress, the John Carter Brown Library, and the libraries of the University of Virginia, University of North Carolina, Princeton University, and the School of Business Administration at Harvard University. Copies of the second edition are in the Library of Congress, John Carter Brown Library, William L. Clements Library, New York Public Library, and the libraries of the University of North Carolina and Harvard University. Copies of the third edition are in the Library of Congress, John Carter Brown Library, and the libraries of Cornell University, Duke University, University of Chicago, University of Virginia, University of Illinois, Harvard

University, and Yale University. Relatively rare, copies of the Norris pamphlet are in the Library of Congress and John Carter Brown Library. This edition is taken from the copies in the John Carter Brown Library.

The pamphlets have been reprinted verbatim with no corrections in spelling or punctuation. [*Sic*] has been used sparingly and only to call attention to misspellings that the reader might find confusing. The marginal headings in the Nairne pamphlet have been placed at the heads of the paragraphs to which they apply. The Norris pamphlet is written in the form of a dialogue. Throughout the last eighty percent of the work, the questions of one party are printed in italics and the answers in roman type. For the first seventeen pages, however, the printer reversed this arrangement. In the interest of clarity, this edition has converted those early pages into the same form as the rest of the work. Original page numbers appear in brackets.

Several people helped with the volume. Richard Waterhouse did the research for most of the annotations many years ago when, shortly after encountering the Norris tract in the John Carter Brown Library in the summer of 1969, I first began to think about publishing it together with the Nairne work in a modern edition. Amy Turner Bushnell read and offered valuable suggestions about the introduction. Kurt Nagel, Grant Mabie, and Steve Young helped to see the volume through the press. Jacqueline Megan Greene did the index. The work was completed while the editor had a fellowship from the National Endowment for the Humanities at the National Humanities Center.

Jack P. Greene
Research Triangle Park
North Carolina
April 14, 1988

Selling
a New World

Introduction:

Early South Carolina and the Psychology of British Colonization

On May 8, 1753, during a debate in the House of Commons at Westminster over a proposed bill to require an annual census of people in Great Britain, the thoughts of several speakers turned to the perennial and, for some people, worrisome questions of how many people were leaving the country every year to settle in the American colonies, why they were going, and whether it was desirable for them to do so. William Thornton, M.P. for York, observed that most emigrants were those who could not "easily find the means of subsistence at home" and asserted that it was far "better [that] they should go and live by their industry there, than that they should live by pilfering, or be supported by their parish at home." Wills Hill, Viscount Hillsborough, M.P. for Warwick, who fifteen years later would become Britain's first secretary of state for the colonies, agreed "that some people go to settle in our colonies because they cannot . . . live at home." But he thought that there was another, equally significant, reason for emigration. "Multitudes of people," he remarked, "go thither yearly, who might live very well at home, and for no other reason but because they hope to live better, or to earn more money in those countries than they can do at home." They were encouraged in this hope, he complained, "by hearing every day of poor people having in a few years got great estates there."[1]

The problem Thornton and Hillsborough addressed in this debate was what might be called the psychology of colonization, a subject that has continued to fascinate students of European expansion down to the present. Except for a few specific sets of data, including the interview statements of emigrants from Britain in the early 1770s recently analyzed in detail by Bernard Bailyn[2] and the testimonies of late seventeenth-century Huguenots captured in flight now being studied systematically for the first time by Neil Kamil,[3] firsthand testimony on the rationale behind the vast transatlantic migration that issued out of Britain and Europe beginning with the early seventeenth century is largely limited to scattered letters and other personal accounts from individual emigrants.

If direct evidence on emigrant motivation is thus fragmentary and random, indirect evidence in the form of contemporary literature about the various colonial enterprises is both extensive and rich, and historians have relied heavily upon it in their efforts to reconstruct the several components of emigrant consciousness. Designed to define for settlers and prospective settlers the true character of these new countries and to explain why people might want to settle there and how the potentialities of these places could best be exploited, this literature included, especially in the case of the earliest colonies, chronicles or histories such as those published by Captain John Smith for Virginia and Richard Ligon for Barbados.[4] More commonly with the many colonies established during the late seventeenth and early eighteenth centuries, however, it consisted almost entirely of descriptive tracts that with few exceptions were unabashedly promotional in their intent.

On the plausible assumption that promotional writers had some clear sense of what their intended audiences might find appealing, scholars of the early modern English colonizing movement have long used the many tracts, pamphlets, and broadsides designed to lure emigrants from the old world to the new as a vehicle for illuminating the psychology of colonization.[5] An especially large promotional literature, heavily concentrated during the first and second generations of settlement, appeared in association with the early years of Virginia during the first half of the seventeenth century, Carolina and Pennsylvania during the late seventeenth and early eighteenth century, and Georgia during the second quarter of the eighteenth century.[6]

For South Carolina, the two fullest, best informed, and most systematic of all the many promotional tracts published about the colony before 1730 appeared early in the second generation of settlement, a full forty years after the foundation of the colony in 1670. First published in London in 1710, *A Letter from South Carolina* was published, also in London, in a second edition in 1718 and a third edition in 1732. All three editions were published anonymously, but the British Library copy of the first edition identifies the author as "Capt. Tho: Nairne a North Brittain," an attribution that has been widely accepted by historians. Whether Nairne was indeed a native Scot or the colonial born son of a Scot is unclear, but he was resident in South Carolina as early as 1698 and subsequently became a large planter near the southernmost area of settlement in Colleton County, which he represented in the elected Commons House of Assembly. In this role, Nairne became a prominent public figure and, as was compatible with his manifestly republican leanings, a powerful advocate of legislative supremacy, regularization of the Indian trade, and toleration of dissenting religion. Sometime agent for the colony in charge of relations with its large and powerful Indian neighbors, Nairne was one of the first victims of the Yamasee War in April 1715. At the time his pamphlet was first published in 1710, he was in London defending himself against charges brought by his political enemy, Governor Sir Nathaniel Johnson.[7] Of uncertain provenance, a manuscript copy of this pamphlet with several notable omissions is in the collections of the John Carter Brown Library in Providence.[8]

The second, considerably longer, and much rarer pamphlet, *Profitable Advice for Rich and Poor*, appeared in London in 1712 and was never reprinted. Although the title page lists no author, an introductory appeal is signed by John Norris, a figure who was far less conspicuous than Nairne in the annals of colonial South Carolina. Indeed, very little is known about him. He was almost certainly from the west of England, probably from the County of Somerset, from where he wrote to the Society for the Propagation of the Gospel in March 1710, and perhaps from Bridgewater, where *Profitable Advice* could be bought from a local bookseller, Robert Davis. In a letter of January 1711 soliciting a position for his son as missionary to the Yamasee Indians, he described himself as "a Planter of South Carolina" who had "settled" in St. Bartholomew's Parish about twenty miles from the Yamasee.

His pamphlet also suggests that he had at least dabbled in various kinds of mercantile activity and had probably been involved with the colony for some time. Also in 1711, Norris published in London an almanac, *The Carolina Calendar for 4 Years, beginning 1712 and ending 1716*, which he described to the Society as the first such publication especially "Calculated for that Province."[9]

Each author identified the ostensible purposes of his tract in a long subtitle. Nairne described his pamphlet as "An Account of the *Soil, Air, Product, Trade, Government, Laws, Religion, People, Military Strength, &c.* of that Province; Together with the Manner and necessary Charges of SETTLING a PLANTATION there, and the *Annual Profit* it will produce." Norris heralded his book as "A Description, or true Relation OF SOUTH CAROLINA, An *English* Plantation, or Colony, in *America*: WITH Propositions for the Advantageous Settlement of People, in General, but especially the Laborious Poor, in that Fruitful, Pleasant, and Profitable Country, for its Inhabitants."[10]

To deliver on the promises explicit in his subtitle, each author employed a familiar literary device. Insisting that he had not written "a regular Treatise," Nairne, assuming the persona of "*a* SWISS *Gentleman*," put his pamphlet in the form of a letter addressed "*to his Friend at* Bern," a place that was then supplying the people for the new settlement of New Bern in North Carolina, and explicitly directed his remarks at disbanded soldiers and mercenaries and possible sponsors of schemes to send such people to the British colonies. Whether Nairne's pamphlet ever reached its intended audience is unclear: it seems to have been translated into neither French nor German. But its initial publication in London renders it probable that Nairne wrote as much for English as for Swiss readers. The fact that the tract subsequently went through two further London editions also suggests that it found a ready audience in England among people who, as Nairne phrased it, "design[ed] to make their Fortunes in new Countries," or were thinking about "transport[ing] themselves [to America] for greater Advantage."[11]

For his part, Norris used the convention of an extended and folksy conversation arising out of a chance meeting between two old friends. Taking on the guise of "*James Freeman, a Carolina* Planter," Norris supplied answers to questions fed to him by

"*Simon Question*, a *West-Country* Farmer." Hoping to hawk his work through such agencies of early modern English social communication as "Town and Country Shopkeepers, Parish-Clerks, Innkeepers, or Masters of Public-Houses," Norris identified the segments of the population that he was trying to reach. First, there were "the honest and laborious poor," including "*Labourers, Men or Women Servants, Boys, Girls, and Children*," as well as the "*Church-Wardens, Over-seers of the Poor, and Paymasters to their Relief*" who, in each parish, were responsible for raising and administering the enormous sums required for poor relief. Second, there were the "*Men of small Estates, or Jusment-Renters*" and "*provident Tradesmen*," "*whose Substance*" was "*small*" and could not live in England "*without hard Labour and Toyl*." Third, there were the "*Rich . . . Merchants, Tradesmen, Gentlemen, Husbandmen, [and] Farmers*," who had "sufficient" estates to fulfill most of their desires but endeavored "for more." Although Norris's description applied to the colony as a whole, he specifically directed potential emigrants to the "Southern Part of *South Carolina*," where he himself had settled in the vicinity of Port Royal and may have had land for sale.[12]

These pamphlets provide a wealth of information about two subjects: first, the psychology and expectations of immigrants who came to the colony, and, second, the nature of what they could expect to find there, including the costs, possible returns, and process of creating a plantation in the lowcountry wilderness during the first decades of the eighteenth century. Those interested in the psychology of colonization during these years will find the nature of the specific appeals made by Nairne and Norris of particular interest, and they wrote in an already well-developed tradition associated with the colony. Not since the establishment of Virginia more than a half century earlier had the founding of any English colony on the North American mainland been so enthusiastically heralded as was that of the new province of Carolina following its creation in the mid-1660s. First settled in 1670, South Carolina, as it would subsequently be called, seemed to be particularly promising. This region, announced the English publicist Richard Blome in 1672, was "generally esteemed one of the best . . . that ever the English were Masters of." Without many of the liabilities English people found so unfamiliar and disorienting in tropical Barbados and Jamaica and with warmer winters than Virginia, South Carolina certainly appeared, as the former proprietor and governor John Archdale remarked in 1707, to have been blessed "in a most peculiar manner" with all "those Temporal Enjoyments that" most "other Nations and Provinces want[ed] the Benefit of." So congenial to vegetation and to animal life were its soil, water, and climate, early promotional writers asserted, that it yielded a rich abundance of all things essential for life. No person could possibly go wanting, and those willing to expend even modest labor could expect to reap substantial fortunes.[13]

"Health, Pleasure, and Profit," declared Blome in first articulating the central theme that would run through virtually all early writings on the colony, could not "be met with in so large measure, in any *Countrey* of the *Indies*." Having surveyed those writings before composing his own proposal for establishing a new colony on the southern border of South Carolina in 1717, Sir Robert Montgomery was impressed by the universal agreement among the authors that South Carolina was "the most amiable Country of the Universe: that Nature has not bless'd the World with any Tract, which can be preferable to it, that *Paradise*, with all her Virgin Beauties, may be modestly suppos'd at most but equal to its Native Excellencies."[14]

Throughout its early history, observers continued to extoll South Carolina as a "Land that flows with Milk and Honey," "the American Canaan" that would certainly in just "a very few years," be "the most useful . . . of all the Plantations upon the continent of America" and, at least in terms of "Agriculture & Tillidge, vye with the Glory of the whole World." Few of South Carolina's early commentators dissented from the judgment that the country, as the Anglican missionary Francis Le Jau succinctly phrased it in early 1707, was "mighty agreable." It was a place, they mostly agreed, that left newcomers "ravisht with Admiration" and so beguiled its new European inhabitants as to establish a permanent claim upon their affections. For nearly a hundred miles back from the seacoast the land was flat and sandy. On first encounter, it conveyed an impression of monotony and barrenness. But closer inspection quickly revealed that, notwithstanding these conditions, it was a natural garden of exceptional beauty and abundance. Wherever settlers looked, reported Robert Ferguson, an associate of one of the Carolina proprietors who himself had never been in the colony, they found "imbellished Meadows, fertil[e], and flourishing Savan[n]a's . . . guarded with pleasant and solitary Woods." Broad grassy plains with few trees, the savannas invited people "to compare *Carolina* to those pleasant Parks [they had left behind] in *England*," while the woods, throughout "beautified with odoriferous and fragrant" plants, were "pleasantly green all the year" and so full of animals and so open that one could there "hunt the Hare, Fox, and Deer all day long in the shade, and freely spur your Horse through the *Woods* to follow the chase."[15]

"Rather . . . a garden than an untilled place," much of South Carolina throughout much of the year appeared "like a bowling alley, full of dainty brooks and rivers of running waters." Even in its natural, unimproved state, Archdale was persuaded, "no Prince in Europe, by all their Art," could "make so pleasant a Sight for the whole Year." "Can Windsor or St[.] James Gardens," the Scottish immigrant John Stewart asked rhetorically in April 1690, "show so much variety, delight, and native fertility even when advanc'd by all that art and wealth can doe, as rude nature spontaneously put[s] forth with us?"[16]

What seemed to make South Carolina "the most Hopeful Settlement the King of *England* has in *America*" and served as its primary appeal to immigrants, however, was less its beauty than its luxuriance. Like Barbados, Jamaica, and Britain's other tropical colonies in the West Indies, it had "always ane thing or other Springing and green all the year long." No other English continental colony in America, not even Virginia, seemed to be so obviously conducive to plant and animal life. South Carolina's rich and well-watered soils and moderate climate, especially its short and mild winters, meant, its proponents said with enthusiasm, that it had "great plenty of all things" necessary for plentiful and easy living. It contained a profusion of timber to use for building houses and shelters and a surplus of game and fish to serve as an instant food supply; and it was suitable for the rapid multiplication of all traditional European domestic animals and the generous growth of both native American and European grains, vegetables, and fruit. "Lying in the very bosom of fruitful

Florida, strech't out on a Bed of Roses so famous and so much celebrated by all the Spanish pens that," one immigrant declared, the colony was "the admiration to every bookishman at Madrid as well as at Charalestoun." South Carolina, in short, appeared to an extravagant degree, as writer after writer declared, to be governed by the "Law of Plenty, extended to the utmost limits of Sanity."[17]

The tracts of both Nairne and Norris represent a perpetuation of this tradition. Yet the fact that writers were still producing promotional tracts forty years after the colony's founding was a testimony less to its success than to its failure. Like those earthly Edens earlier forecast for Virginia, Barbados, Jamaica, and other colonies, this newest American paradise did not immediately fulfill the promise suggested by its rich natural endowments. Notwithstanding the rapid emergence of livestock as an easy road to economic competence in the 1670s and 1680s and the development of rice as a profitable agricultural staple in the 1690s, hostile neighbors, ineffective governing institutions, ill-health, hot summers, serious shortages of labor and capital, internal religious and political divisions among Anglicans and dissenters and between rival ethnic and economic groups, and perhaps the colony's predominantly slave labor system all combined to give South Carolina a highly negative image as a hot, unhealthy, dangerous, disorderly, and crude society and thereby to discourage immigration and retard the colony's growth. Lagging far behind that of Pennsylvania which had been founded a decade later, its population in 1710 included at most no more than 5,000 to 6,000 settlers of European descent and perhaps a similar number of African slaves, and they were very thinly scattered over a small area within twenty to forty miles of the seacoast.[18]

Neither Nairne nor Norris denied that South Carolina was in many respects a "Strange Country" with many continuing problems. Like their predecessors, however, they concentrated upon its extraordinary material promise. Endeavoring to counter its negative reputation in Britain, they depicted it—in terms that seemed to them best calculated to entice immigrants to come to South Carolina—as a safe and inviting place where there was virtually no poverty, people could live in plenty with little labor, and riches were easily accessible to the industrious.[19]

What they primarily stressed was the astonishing ease with which people in South Carolina could live and accumulate wealth. There was "no Place in the Continent of *America*," Nairne wrote, "where People can transport themselves to greater Advantage." "With moderate Industry," he observed, a person could "be supplied with all the Necessaries of Life." South Carolina, Norris agreed, was a place where people could not only "live with greater Plenty and Content" than ever they could in England but also "advance themselves in Riches, Honour, and good Repute" and in just a "few Years become of good Substance and Worth." Whereas a large proportion of the English population had to live in "Scarcity, Poverty, and Want," no one in South Carolina, Nairne insisted, was "obliged to beg for want of food" except "Widows or Children of such Strangers, who die[d] before they" were "comfortably settled." Norris echoed this judgement. South Carolina had no poor rates, Norris assured his readers, because free people could "forthwith imploy themselves so Advantageously to their own Benefit, for themselves, or under some other Planter, that they need not any such supply." Nor, Norris insisted, was opportunity for betterment limited to the poor. In England, he contended, even men with some resources were "never like to be in a Capacity of otherwise Advancing their Fortune from their present State and Condition they are now in, to any higher Degree of Riches, Content, or Repute." By contrast, South Carolina presented them with "the Opportunity . . . of Benefiting themselves, during the Remainder of their life."[20]

What made South Carolina such a land of opportunity for all classes of prospective immigrants was cheap land, fertile soil, and natural abundance. "Nothing can be more reasonable," Nairne wrote, "than the Price of Lands" which, he emphasized, were held in "Free and common Soccage" with only "a small Quit-Rent being paid annually to the Proprietors." As "an Encouragement to People to resort thither," Norris pointed out, the proprietors had deliberately made lands available *on very easy and cheap Terms.* One hundred acres, he reported, could be bought for less than ten acres in England. Moreover, even an impecunious servant who had finished his term could "have Land assign'd him from the Lords Proprietors."[21]

Land was not only cheap and accessible but also extraordinarily fecund. Producing "the best *Rice* that is brought to *England* from any Part of the World," the soil of the colony was so prolific that agricultural yields were much "greater than . . . in *England*." "Ten Acres there, well Husbanded in [rice, the] proper Grain of that Country," according to Norris, generated "more Profit than Twenty Acres" in England cultivated according to "the general Way of Husbandry." A half bushel of corn and peas to an acre routinely yielded 12 to 15 bushels of peas and 20 or 25 bushels of corn, and some people got as much as 20 bushels of peas and 40 bushels of corn. One good laboring man, Norris asserted, could in a year clear, fence, plant, hoe, harvest, and thresh at least four acres of corn and peas besides land planted with food for the family's use and three acres of rice, an acre of which was "as Valuable as two or three Acres of *English* Grain." With such "Fertile Soil," any "Laborious and Industrious Man, being settled for himself," could, merely "with his own Labour and Industry, [easily] maintain a Wife and Ten Children, sufficient with *Corn, Pease, Rice, Flesh, Fish, and Fowl*." Having many other marketable products and foodstuffs generated by the colony's natural abundance, including naval stores and cattle, with which South Carolina abounded "to a Degree much beyond any other *English* Colony," and stocked with large quantities of wood, fish, and game that, in contrast to England, was not reserved to the wealthy by game laws, South Carolina was obviously "*a very plentiful Country for Food*" and other essentials, a place where people could escape poverty and want and "*live well*" and "in great Affluence of most things necessary for Life."[22]

The argument that immigrants in such a yielding and beneficent environment could scarcely avoid improving their material circumstances while those who desired riches were virtually assured of success was the main theme in the works of both Nairne and Norris and a reiteration of what had been an important component in the colony's appeal from its first foundation. For those who, already having some resources, were interested in the "Advancement of their Fortunes," Norris wrote, no country offered better prospects. Except for "Gentlemen of Great Estates, or great Userers," he believed, every category of independent people could by settling in South Carolina "advance and prefer themselves to a [vastly] more plentiful and profitable Way to Live" than they could ever do in England.[23]

Both Nairne and Norris refined and considerably expanded upon John Archdale's calculation in an earlier promotional pamphlet, published in 1707, that, with prudent management, a man with £500 to invest could, "in a few Years, live in as much Plenty, yea more, than a Man of 300£ a Year in England; and if he continue[s] Careful . . . shall increase to great Wealth[,] as many there are already Witnesses." Whereas a person in England with £1,000 sterling to invest could expect a return of only about £50 a year, Nairne estimated that in South Carolina a similar sum would enable a person to establish a well-equipped thousand-acre estate with thirty slaves that would yield annual profits of nearly £340. Similarly, Norris calculated that the same sum would permit the foundation of a working plantation of between one thousand and fifteen hundred acres with thirty-six slaves producing yearly returns of at least £400. With such high profits, almost six to eight times what could be expected in England, a planter, in Norris's words, could acquire "great quantities of Land as well as Stock" and many slaves who could in turn be employed in planting corn and rice and making naval stores to the "great Profit and Advantage" of their masters, who, "in Time, [would] thereby become able to build fine Brick Houses" and otherwise maintain their families *"with Credit and Honour."*[24]

But one did not have to have such a large sum to do well in South Carolina. With only £100 sterling to invest, enough, by Nairne's figures, to buy two slaves and 200 acres and, by Norris's calculations, to purchase three slaves and 150 acres, a man could settle comfortably and eventually "get a competent Estate, and live very handsom[e]ly." Those with still less who could pay their own passage or even had to go as servants had several avenues by which they could rise in the world. Either they could work for wages and thereby get £25 or £30 per year, a rate much higher than they could obtain in England, or they could work as shareholders on terms favorable enough to give them housing, food, and up to half of all the produce they made in return for nothing more than their labor. Alternatively, with credit for all the "necessary Implements" easily obtainable from local merchants, Nairne explained, individuals could simply occupy "a Piece of Ground, improve it, build, raise, stock, plant Orchards, and make such Commodities, which being sold, procur'd . . . Slaves, Horses, Hous[e]hold-Goods, and the like Conveniencies; and after this was done, in seven or eight Years . . . to think it Time to pay the Lords something for their Land."[25]

Whatever route they chose, whether by squatting and improving a piece of land to which they did not have title or by working for another man for wages or shares, both Nairne and Norris emphasized, a poor, diligent, and "careful Man and his Wife" could in "a few Years" become "Masters and Owners of Plantations, Stocks, & Slaves, on which they [could] Live very plentifully." "I knew a Man, that at his first coming into the Country, was a Servant for Four Years," Norris explained, "yet before his Death, it was computed [that] he had at least Three Thousand Head of Cattle, Young and Old; and a Hundred Horses; and Three Hundred Calves Yearly." Indeed, he reported, "many Men" who could scarcely purchase a cow or two "at their first beginning" had merely "by their Stocks of Cattle and Hogs, in a few Years, become Rich" and were then "settle[d] well on a Plantation of their own." Only lazy people, intemperate drinkers, or "extravagant, careless, and bad Husbands" could fail to succeed in the rich and bountiful environment of South Carolina.[26]

Although South Carolina was especially advantageous for husbandmen and planters, it also held out bright prospects to those in nonagricultural employment. By English standards, artisans could command extravagant wages, which Nairne listed for several of the most prominent categories of tradesmen, while most merchants who settled in Charleston "with a quantity of Goods," including both importers and shopkeepers, could expect, "as many there have done," to "grow very Rich, in a few Years . . . from a small Beginning." Those traders who were willing to settle "with good Stocks of Goods . . . to furnish the Inhabitants, and *Indian* Traders" in the new town of Port Royal, which Norris predicted would soon "become a Place of great Trade," could expect to do even better, "soon grow[ing] extreamly Rich, as many Merchants, Shopkeepers, and others did, at the first settling their Trade in that Town, and doth still so continue getting Riches, to Admiration, many of them now being worth many *Thousand Pounds*, from a very small Beginning." A mercantile partnership that could put together ten to twelve thousand pounds of goods, Norris predicted, "might clearly get . . . (with good Success at Sea) at least 5 or 6000*l*. on their Returns" every year.[27]

What greatly enhanced the prospects of escaping want and acquiring wealth in South Carolina, both Nairne and Norris emphasized, was the simplicity and cheapness of government. Compared with England, the public realm was minute. The civil establishment was small. The members of the governor's executive council and the legislature received no "allowance for attending publick Service, but" served "at their own Expence," and the only public officials who received a salary were the governor and ten ministers of the Church of England. With little poverty, the colony had no expenses for maintaining the poor. With "no regular troops in *Carolina*, except a very few in the Fort, and Sentinals in several Places along the Coast," defense costs, even including fortifications built to protect the colony against invasion by the Spaniards, were low. Altogether, Nairne reported, the public expenses were less than £3,500 a year. Moreover, the representatives of the freeholders in the legislature, Nairne pointed out, scrupulously kept the appointment of all revenue collectors in legislative hands, gave no discretionary spending power to proprietary governors, and required a strict accounting of any disbursements of public funds. "Frugality being a Vertue very useful in large Governments," Nairne remarked, was "absolutely necessary in small and poor ones."[28]

All of these conditions meant both that there were "very few Countries where public Credit" was "better preserved than" in South Carolina and that taxes were exceedingly low. Indeed, as Nairne pointed out, there were not yet any "Taxes in *South Carolina*, either upon real or personal Estates" and the public revenues were supplied wholly by duties on imports and exports, which he claimed produced nearly twenty-five percent more in funds than were needed to meet public costs. With such low "common Publick Taxes on the Province," the proportion of private income that went for public expenditures, Norris declared in underlining a point he made over and over, was "very small" in comparison "with what they are in *England*." In England, he wrote, the "many Taxes, Rates, Assessments, and other Disbursements" to which "all Estates" were liable were so high that they took "away *one* Half, if not two Thirds, of the Value" of annual returns and thereby rendered impossible even for "an *Industrious* Man" to accumulate much profit from "his own laborious Care and Industry." By contrast, low public expenditures in South Carolina meant that people there did not have "to straighten themselves . . . Quarterly, or oftener, to pay great Taxes, Rates[,] Rents, and Assessments" and that there were "*few Occasions for the Planter to expend his Profits that arises from his Labour.*" As a consequence, Norris asserted, a family in South Carolina had a better chance both to obtain all "*reasonable Necessaries from their own Industry*" and to "*live very plentiful[,] . . . thrive in the World, and become Rich.*"[29]

Nairne and Norris thus summoned people to South Carolina by what David Bertelson has called the doctrine of allurement, the prospects that its extraordinary material promise would enable them to live there without want in ease and abundance and perhaps even become rich. Every species of person, Norris proclaimed, "*Rich and Poor, Merchants, Tradesmen, Gentlemen, Husbandmen, Farmers, Labourers, Men or Women Servants, Boys, Girls, and Children*" could in South Carolina expect to improve their material circumstances and to rise in the world. To "*live . . . Plentiful, and get Riches withal to Admiration,*" these were the primary appeals employed by Nairne and Norris to persuade people to immigrate to the colony and probably also the major considerations in the decisions of immigrants to come.[30]

But these were by no means the only attractions held out by Nairne and Norris. Also important was the possibility that wealth in South Carolina could be acquired with relatively little labor. They did not claim that riches could "be got without Industry." But they did argue, in Nairne's words, that in South Carolina "as little will serve to put a Person into a Way of living comfortably, as in any Place whatever, and perhaps less." What made this fetching situation possible was not just the colony's natural abundance which made the work even of servants and slaves much less onerous than "that [of] many Thousand[s of] Servants and poor Laboure[r]s . . . in *England, Wales, Scotland,* and *Ire-*

land" but the institution of slavery itself. Far from condemning slavery, Nairne and Norris, like most of their British contemporaries, presented it as a boon to independent families. Employable "in any sort of Labour, either in Town or Country, in whatever their Masters, or Owners, have occasion to be done," slaves offered several advantages over servants or hired labor. "With good Management and Success," Norris pointed out, "a Man's Slave will by his Labour, pay for his first Cost in about Four Years at most, besides his Maintenance," which did not cost much, slaves largely feeding themselves and requiring but little clothing. Moreover, because masters had "as good a Right and Title to them, during their Lives, as a Man has here to a Horse or Ox, after he has bought them," every slave's labor, once his initial cost had been recovered, was "free Gain" for "the Remainder of his Life." As much as anything else, Norris thus suggested, slavery enabled people in South Carolina to live easily "without being oblig'd to Labour themselves, as most Jusment-renters are here, or Men of small Estates."[31]

As important as the prospect of escaping poverty, rising above meanness, and obtaining wealth and substance with little labor was in the appeals of both Nairne and Norris, neither seems to have presented it as an end in itself. Rather, material betterment was for each the vehicle by which *dependent* men in Britain and Europe could become *independent*, masterless men with dependents of their own in South Carolina. Free people were uninterested in working for wages for others, Norris reported, because, "by Planting . . . Corn and Rice" on "their own Land," they could "employ themselves very advantageously in their own Business." "How much better for Men to improve their own Lands, for the Use of themselves, and Posterity; to sit under their own Vine, and eat the Fruits of their Labour," than to work for others, declared Nairne, invoking a popular biblical metaphor. In a place where the road to independence and a comfortable subsistence was so open, Norris observed, people soon came to rely entirely upon themselves and to scorn charity. In South Carolina, he wrote, "I never yet saw . . . any Family so Poor and in Want, but that, if a small Gift of any kind of Provisions was offer'd them, because 'twas suppos'd they could not subsist without such Helps, they would refuse it, and scorn the Acceptance thereof." If few people in the colony had yet acquired large fortunes, Nairne wrote, most people quickly and easily had been able to achieve "that State of Life which many People reckon the happiest, a moderate Subsistance, without a Vexation of Dependance."[32]

But the prospects of obtaining wealth with ease and escaping the dependence that was the lot of the vast majority of the population of England would have meant little in a menacing environment, and both Nairne and Norris took pains to minimize the unpleasant and dangerous features that already had combined to give South Carolina an ambiguous reputation. They had to admit that throughout the summer temperatures were "indeed troublesome to Strangers." But they contended that settlers had quickly found satisfactory remedies in the form of "open airy Rooms, Arbours and Summer-houses" constructed in shady groves and frequent cool baths and insisted that the discomfitures of the summers were more than offset by the agreeableness of the rest of the seasons. Similarly, they denied that there was much danger from any of the terrifying creatures who made the colony their habitat. Despite having names that were "frightful to those who never saw them," alligators, wolves, panthers, bears, and other wild animals usually tried to avoid people unless attacked, while the woods contained an effective antidote to the poisonous venom of the rattlesnake, the "most dangerous Creature" in the colony. Finally, Nairne and Norris tried to counter reports, which were all too accurate, about the colony's seemingly increasingly malignant disease environment, suggesting that ill-health was largely limited to newcomers before they were seasoned to the climate, to people who insisted upon living in low marshy ground, and to those who were excessive and careless in their eating, drinking, and personal habits. "If temperate," they asserted, those who lived on "dry healthy Land," were "generally, very healthful."[33]

Discomfiting summers, strange and ferocious animals and serpents, and ill health were of course little more dangerous than the risks of war and destruction arising out of South Carolina's proximity to colonies of England's European rivals, Spanish Florida and French Louisiana, and its growing commercial involvement with the many powerful Indian nations in south-eastern North America. Except for a brief Spanish foray into the southern portion of the colony in 1686 and some occasional skirmishes on the frontier between Carolina Indian traders and their French and Spanish rivals, South Carolina had been free from invasion throughout its early history. Indeed, during the early years of Queen Anne's War, South Carolinians had actually carried the attack to their foreign neighbors with a partially successful expedition against the Spanish capital of Florida at St. Augustine in 1702 and a victorious thrust against them at Apalache in 1704. In 1706, moreover, they had managed to drive off a joint Franco-Spanish invasion force.[34]

Although they remained anxious about the possibility of Franco-Spanish retaliation until the conclusion of war in 1713, these early military successes seem to have contributed to a growing self-confidence and to have demonstrated the efficacy of the militia system. Denouncing professional armies as "Instruments in the Hands of Tyrants, to ravage and depopulate the Earth," Nairne did not deny that South Carolinians had to be concerned with defense. Rather, he argued that every "Planter who keeps his Body fit for Service, by Action and a regular Life" was the military superior of every regular soldier "whose Spirits and Vigour are soon pall'd by an idle effeminate Life, in a warm Climate." Praising the expertise of native white Carolinians in the use of firearms, a skill "very well . . . acquir'd by the frequent Pursuit of Game in the Forests," Nairne, writing in the English republican tradition associated with the political philosopher James Harrington, extolled the virtues of a citizen army. Carolinians, he observed, had "the same Opinion of Arms as the *Romans*, and other free People, generally had," believing that no one was "so fit to defend their Properties as themselves." To enjoy "the many Pleasures and Delights of a quiet peaceable Life," a "free People, surrounded with potent Neighbours," he insisted, had to take responsibility "for their own Defence" and therefore needed "to be brave, and military, [and] perfectly vers'd in Arms."[35]

As proof of the efficacy of the militia system and the colony's safety, Nairne pointed to the fact that Carolinians solely by their own exertions had "intirely broke and ruin'd the Strength of the *Spaniards* in *Florida*, destroy'd the whole Country, burnt the Towns, brought all the *Indians*, who were not kill'd or made

Slaves, into our Territories, so that there is not now, so much as one Village with ten Houses in it, in all *Florida*, that is subject to the *Spaniards*." By thus "reducing *Spanish* Power in *Florida* so low, that they are altogether incapable of ever harming us" and "by training our *Indian* Subjects in the Use of Arms, and Knowledge of War, which would be of Service to us, in case of any Invasion," these expeditions, Nairne explained, had along with "strong and regular Works" built to fortify Charleston "added very much to our Strength and Safety."[36]

Nairne and Norris thus appealed to prospective settlers on the grounds that they could live in South Carolina in abundance, ease, independence, and safety; equally important, they also argued that the colony was a society that was rapidly becoming more cultivated and improved, another new Albion on the western shores of the Atlantic. The people who created and perpetuated the new societies of colonial British America sought not merely wealth and personal independence as individuals and the welfare of their families but also the social goal of improved societies that would both guarantee the independence they hoped to achieve and enable them to enjoy its fruits. Indeed, demands and aspirations for improvement were nearly as prominent in the promotional literature as were those for affluence and independence. Ubiquitous in the economic writings of early modern Britain, the language of improvement primarily referred to schemes, devices, or projects through which the economic position of the nation might be advanced, the estates or fortunes of individuals bettered, or existing resources made more productive.[37]

In the new and relatively undeveloped societies of colonial British America, the term *improvement* carried similar connotations but it also acquired a much wider meaning. It was used to describe a state of society that was far removed from the savagery associated with that "Primitive Race of Mankind," the native Indians. An *improved* society was one defined by a series of negative and positive juxtapositions. Not wild, barbaric, irregular, rustic, or crude, it was settled, cultivated, civilized, orderly, developed, and polite, and the primary model for an improved society was the emerging and more settled, orderly, coherent, and developed society of contemporary Britain.[38]

Neither Nairne nor Norris argued that South Carolina was yet a fully improved and anglicized society. Indeed, they both took pains to point out the many differences between the colony and its metropolitan model. The most striking difference was in the composition of the labor force. Because servants were so difficult to procure and slavery was a more profitable form of labor, most of "the Business of the Country," including all of "the greatest Drudgeries," was performed by black and Indian slaves, and servants were "seldom put to other Employments than to exercise some Trade, oversee a Plantation, or to carry Goods to Market." As a result, only about twelve percent of the total population was of European descent, twenty-two percent was black, and a whopping sixty-six percent were still "*Indian* subjects." Agricultural units were not called farms but plantations, and estate owners not farmers but planters, and the short and mild winters meant that the agricultural cycle was different "in all Respects from Seed-Time 'till Harvest." The great many stumps remaining in the fields after they had been cleared prevented the use of ploughs, neither orchards nor vineyards were "yet common," few planters produced much butter or cheese, and English grain was neglected in favor of rice because it was much less profitable, an acre of rice being "as Valuable as two or three Acres of *English* Grain." The intensity of the summer heat forced people to "leave their Labour" and confine themselves to the shade for "Three or Four Hours in the Middle of the Day . . . and Refresh and Divert themselves in Bathing in Cool-Water; and retiring to the Shady Groves, Arbours, or Houses." For the same reason, for the "greatest Part of the Year" most people went "very thin clad, and airy," making their clothing half cotton instead of all wool as was the custom in England. The absence of building stone forced people to build their houses and other buildings with either brick or timber.[39]

If these many differences were ones to which most immigrants could easily adapt, there were still others that, in the eyes of Nairne and Norris, made South Carolina clearly superior to Britain. The greater productivity of the soil meant that agricultural yields were considerably higher and that there was no need to manure it. Domestic animals of all sorts—cattle, hogs, and fowl—were much more prolific, and there were no game laws.

Still other areas of obvious superiority included those that had been deliberately built in to the institutions of the colony by its early leaders. As Daniel Defoe remarked in a pamphlet published in 1705, the proprietors of Carolina had consciously set out to build a colony "upon some better Foundations . . . than the rest of the English Colonies." What Defoe specifically had in mind and what Nairne and Norris also emphasized were the provisions that people of all Protestant religious persuasions were to "have free *Toleration* to exercise and enjoy the same without Interruption" and that "All foreign Protestants, of what Denomination soever," were to be "made Denizens within three Months after their Arrival." Following revocation of the Edict of Nantes, these provisions, Nairne noted, attracted large numbers of French Huguenots who "live[d] in good Friendship with . . . the *English*" and "contributed not a little to improve the Country." With forty percent Anglicans, twenty percent Presbyterians, twenty percent French Calvinists, ten percent Anabaptists, and ten percent Quakers and others, the religious diversity of the settler population, Norris suggested, testified to the success of this policy. Nor was the religious area the only one in which South Carolina had shown some improvement over the society of metropolitan Britain. "In several things," Nairne observed, citing as evidence the choosing of juries by ballot from among a select list "of all the best qualified Persons in the Country," "we have . . . refin'd upon the *English* Laws."[40]

Notwithstanding these many differences between South Carolina and Britain, the message projected by both Nairne and Norris was that during its brief existence South Carolina had become increasingly English. If its new European inhabitants had taken an area that had lain "for several Ages of Time unimprov'd and neglected," they had quickly transformed it into a country that, "in proportion to the Length of time, and Stock of *English* Mon[e]y originally expended in Settling it," was, as Nairne contended, "much better improv'd than any other *English* colony on the Continent of *America*." The landscape was being increasingly anglicized, trade was expanding rapidly, and they had already created a settled and hierarchical social structure dominated by the planters, who, composing eighty-five percent of the independent white population, like the English gentry, lived "by their own and their Servants['] Industry, improve[d] their Estates, follow[ed] Tillage or Grasing, and" made "those Commodities which are transported from hence to *Great Britain,* and other Places," to the great profit of themselves and the colony. Moreover, since the legislature had "divided the Inhabited Part of the Country into Parishes, and caus'd Churches . . . and Parsonage-Houses" to be built with two to three hundred acres of glebe land attached to them, the colony had attracted many ministers of the established church and had fifteen ministers of all denominations.[41]

With stronger and more plentiful religious institutions, Nairne wrote proudly, "Religion and Piety have increas'd and flourished among us, in good Measure," a development that, he thought, had in turn "greatly contributed to the Good of Society, by refining those Dispositions which were otherwise rude and untractable." Indeed, he insisted, the *"European* Inhabitants of the Province" were, "for the most part, People of Sobriety and Industry" who were both "very temperate, and have generally an Aversion to excessive Drinking." Without "that Moroseness and Sullenness of Temper, so common in other Places," South Carolinians, according to Nairne, retained all the best characteristics of English people. "Very . . . liberal in assisting" newcomers, orphans, and unfortunates, "no People," he averred, were "more hospitable, generous, and willing to do good Offices to Strangers; every one is ready to entertain them freely, with the best they have." Nor were they in any way a dull people. Rather, they were mostly "ingenious, of good Capacities, and quick Apprehensions, and have Heads excellently well turn'd for mechanical Works and Inventions." "With little or no teaching," he observed, "they'll make Houses, Mills, Sloops, Boats, and the like."[42]

Not surprisingly, South Carolina by the early eighteenth century also had "many wise & honest men" to attend to the public service. For "the better and more effectual Preservation of the Lives and Estates of the Inhabitants," Nairne reported, the colony's early leaders had taken full advantage of the "generous Principles of civil and religious Liberty" offered by the proprietors to institute a government that in form was "as nigh as convenient can be to that of *England*," with representative institutions and guarantees of English liberties and English laws. From these "noble Foundation[s]," they and their successors had gradually fashioned an admirable constitution by which "known Laws" were the sole "Measure and Bounds of Power" and liberty was "so well and legally established" that no laws or regulations could be enforced without the explicit sanction of the representatives of the citizens meeting in an elected assembly modeled "as nigh as possible" after the British House of Commons. This assembly, moreover, not only "claim[ed] all the Power, Priviledges, and Immunities, which the House of Commons, have in Great Britain" but also took pains to "retain that Power they have by Law, and preserve the just Ballance of the Government." As if to symbolize their deep commitment to the establishment of a government of laws, a courthouse had been the first public building erected by South Carolina's earliest leaders, and they ever after, Nairne approvingly told his readers, took pains to provide proper officers and courts that would insure impartial administration of justice. In just a few decades, Nairne and Norris thus argued, British settlers in South Carolina had managed to create a civilized British society with a system of governance every bit as conducive to order, liberty, and security of property as that of the metropolis itself and a liberal religious climate in which people of all Protestant faiths could feel comfortable.[43]

Notwithstanding these several evidences of the anglicization of the South Carolina social landscape, neither Nairne nor Norris suggested that South Carolina was yet the fully improved English society its settlers had hoped to build. Like the earlier promotional writer Robert Ferguson, they could point with pride "to the Growth, Conveniency, and Manufacture of the Country; the Regularity of Living, and Reformation of Life: the Medium of Manners, and the good and happy issues of Prosperity to the Settlement." They could also look forward to the time when, in Ferguson's words, the colony would "grow up to such compleat maturity" that it would finally "bring forth more *Cicero's*, than boasting Thraso's." But they could not argue that South Carolina yet "abound[ed] with those gay and noisie amusements" or that richly textured social, cultural, and political life characteristic of the urban centers and densely populated rural areas of contemporary Britain.[44]

Seeking to make a virtue of the colony's still primitive social character, Nairne and Norris depicted it as a new Arcadia that offered "a safe and pleasant Retreat" from the bustle of so much of metropolitan Britain, the perfect place for those who took pleasure in the "innocent Delights of plain simple Nature" and could be content with "a Blissful, Retir'd Country Life" of "Solitude, Contemplation, Planting, Gardening, Orchards, Groves, Woods, Fishing, Fowling, [and] Hunting Wild Beasts." If South Carolina did not yet have the dense society and cultural amenities suitable for satisfying the tastes of the "great and [the] rich" of Britain, they observed, there was no better place in all of the British dominions for those who had "experienc'd the Frowns of Fortune . . . to make a handsome Retreat from the World." With only a small public stage, this "remote Country," both writers emphasized, was perfect for people who preferred to seek their happiness in the private realm. In contrast to Britain, there was not that "Multiplicity of Publick Affairs to molest or disturb" a man's "quiet innocent Pleasure." Even the method of jury selection prevented any "one set of Persons" from being "too much burthen'd" by that essential public obligation but insured that "all should have an equal Share of the Trouble." With so few public duties, every man could concentrate upon his own private affairs, thus insuring that he would "with moderate Industry be supplied with all the Necessaries of Life" and "plentifully enjoy the Fruits of his Diligence, and Delight, in Improvements, on a large and pleasant Plantation, adorn'd . . . with Buildings, Fish-Ponds, Park, Warren, Gardens, Orchards, or whatever else best delights him" in the full enjoyment of his "Family, Neighbours, and Friends, with all the innocent, delightful Satisfaction imaginable." A man who could be happy with a quiet peaceable life and wanted nothing more than simply to improve his estate for the benefit of himself and his posterity, they suggested, could live "with greater Content" in South Carolina than anywhere in the contemporary British world.[45]

The promise for individuals of a quiet, regular, abundant, and comfortable life in surroundings that were becoming increasingly British was the primary but by no means the only motive cited by Norris and Nairne for emigrating to South Carolina. By pursuing *"their own Private Interest,"* they suggested, immigrants would unavoidably also contribute to the *"Publick Good"* of the entire British nation. Both writers stressed the potential national and public benefits of emigration. Norris explicitly heralded emigration as a device for taking poor families off the poverty rolls and thereby reducing local expenditures for poor relief and providing members of an unproductive segment of the population with the opportunity to contribute both to their own support and to the wealth of the nation. In an attempt to interest the Carolina proprietors and the British Board of Trade in a scheme to provide public money to assist emigrants, Nairne even supplied precise calculations of the specific returns that might be expected from an investment of £6,000 to transport and settle ninety laboring men in South Carolina. Estimating that each of these people would "add 5*l.* yearly to the Wealth of *Great Britain*" and would soon be employing at least four slaves, each of whom would add an equal amount, Nairne calculated the annual return from them for the nation at £2,250 at the end of seven years and £3,375 at the end of twenty years. On the basis of these rough figures, Nairne projected a total return to Britain during the first twenty years of over £36,000. Adding this figure to the value of estates in land and slaves created by these settlers, which he estimated at £67,500, Nairne put the total yield for the first twenty years at slightly more than £104,000, almost seventeen times the amount of the original investment. At the same time, according to Nairne, that investment would have added 225 families to the colony's settler population, brought 44,800 acres of land under occupation, and produced yearly quitrents to the proprietors in excess of £300.[46]

Whatever returns additional settlers in South Carolina might bring to the British nation, the colony's main attraction as depicted by Nairne and Norris was the promise it held for individual immigrants and settlers to advance themselves and their families economically and socially, and they filled their tracts with a variety of data and advice on what economic resources, tools, labor, and provisions were necessary to establish a plantation, what procedures ought to be followed to make a plantation profitable, and what returns settlers might expect from their investments of money and labor. Both writers offered data on the establishment costs, necessary items, and rates of return for a plantation with initial investments of £100 and £1,000 sterling. Both authors proffered advice on the best time and methods of settling and information on the proper seasons for sowing and harvest, the usual yields of corn, peas, and rice, and techniques for producing rice, silk, rosin, tar, and pitch, none of which were familiar to most English farmers. Nairne offered data on wages for several kinds of employment, and Norris described in detail the terms on which impecunious emigrants might get passage to the colony and provided information on the cost of transport: £7 from London and £5 to £6 from the outports of Bristol, Bideford, Exeter, Topsham, and Liverpool. This information constitutes some of the most detailed and authoritative evidence available on these subjects for late proprietary South Carolina.[47]

With £100 for an initial investment, both authors calculated that a family could live, in Nairne's words, "with Comfort and Decency." According to Nairne, that sum would purchase two hundred acres of land, two black slaves, four cows and calves, four sows, a canoe, a steel mill for grinding corn, and all the food and tools, including axes, hoes, wedges, hand saws, and hammers necessary to build a small temporary house and to clear enough land to become self-sufficient in foodstuffs by the end of the year with nearly £10 left for other contingent expenses. For the same amount, Norris calculated that a couple could buy the same items promised by Nairne plus six ewes and a ram, sixteen "good Cows and Calves, and a Bull," an unspecified number of breeding poultry, and all the equipment necessary to enable the wife to produce butter and cheese with less than £7 left for unforeseen expenses.[48]

For £1,000 a family could establish a magnificent estate. By Nairne's estimate, that sum would buy 1,000 acres of land; a labor force consisting of thirty black slaves equally divided between men and women; a vast stock, including twenty cows and calves, three horses, six sows and a boar, and ten ewes and a ram; a large pirogue and a small canoe for water transportation; a steel mill and all the tools, ploughs, and carts necessary to clear and plant ninety acres of land, half of it in rice, and to build a small house; and enough provisions to feed the family and slaves for the first year with nearly £25 left over for contingencies. Such an estate, according to Nairne, would return over £300 annually. By

Norris's calculations, the same sum would buy between 1,000 and 1,500 acres with a labor force of thirty-six slaves, including fifteen black men, three black women, and eighteen Indian women; livestock consisting of thirty cows and calves and two bulls, three horses, six sows and a boar, twenty ewes and a ram, four oxen, and "Fowls of several Sorts for to kill, and also to bred from"; a large pirogue, a small canoe, and carts for transportation of goods and produce; the tools needed to clear and plant ninety acres, sixty in rice and thirty in corn and peas; a year's provisions and dairy equipment; and the labor for carpenters to produce a small house, with over £60 left for contingencies. Such an estate, Norris predicted, would yield £400 per year, a quarter more than promised by Nairne.[49]

Both Nairne and Norris advocated beginning this process in the early fall. By immigrating in September, they agreed, an immigrant gave himself, as Nairne put it, "eight Months moderate Weather" in which to acclimate himself to the climate "before the Heat comes." But September was also the best time to start a plantation because it gave the planter up to six months to clear land at the rate of about three acres per laboring hand, build shelters for his slaves and family, and fence his corn ground before it was time to plant about March 1. If the first year was thus spent clearing land, constructing shelter, and planting essential crops to feed and return a small profit for the plantation, the second was the time both to clear more land and to make gardens, plant orchards, and build barns and other necessary buildings, while the third and fourth winters could be employed in clearing still more land and building a more substantial house for the planter, the original house thenceforth serving as a kitchen and the more substantial planters building their new dwellings of brick. In just three or four years, according to both authors, new settlers could be living in a plentiful and comfortable way, free of the "Scarcity, Poverty, and Want" the poorest of them had known in the old country and with every prospect of obtaining wealth, substance, and honor in their new country.[50]

Nairne and Norris thus beckoned people to South Carolina to pursue their own individual happinesses. They either minimized or sought to translate into advantages the several conditions that had operated to prevent the colony from developing more rapidly during its first four decades—its malignant disease environment, hot summers, divisive public life, cultural crudeness, and situation close to powerful Indian nations and the colonies of hostile European powers. Above all, they sought to depict South Carolina as a place where immigrants could find "a more plentiful and profitable Way to Live." In articulating this vision, in inviting prospective immigrants "to go thither to advance themselves," Nairne and Norris appealed to what appears to have been the most powerful animating impulse in the thousands of individual decisions by early modern Britons and Europeans to pull up stakes in the old world and move to the new: the desire to begin anew in a place with manifold opportunities for individual economic and social advancement in which—in the new field of action that was America—men might be active agents in their quest for competence, substance, independence, and the capacity to shape their own lives however they wanted. That, at least insofar as Nairne and Norris perceived the situation, those goals had to be achieved through the systematic subjugation of dependent African and Indian slaves was far less of a disincentive to immigration than readers with modern sensibilities might suppose.[51]

NOTES

1. Speeches of Thornton and Hillsborough, May 8, 1753, in Leo F. Stock, ed., *Proceedings and Debates of the British Parliament respecting North America*, 5 vols. (Washington, D.C., 1924–41), V, 567–68.
2. Bernard Bailyn, *Voyagers to the West: A Passage in the Peopling of America on the Eve of the Revolution* (New York, 1986).
3. Neil Kamil, "Reformation, Natural Science, and the Foundations of Artisanal Thought in Colonial America: La Rochelle, New York City, and the Huguenot Paradigm, 1517–1740," unpublished PhD. diss., Johns Hopkins University 1988.
4. See John Smith, *The Generall History of Virginia, the Somers Iles, and New England* (London, 1623), and Richard Ligon, *A True & Exact History of the Island of Barbadoes* (London, 1657).
5. Among the best examples are Howard Mumford Jones, "The Colonial Impulse: An Analysis of the Promotion Literature of Colonization," *Proceedings of the American Philosophical Society*, 90 (1946): 131–61, and Hugh T. Lefler, "Promotional Literature of the Southern Colonies," *Journal of Southern History*, 33 (1967): 3–25.
6. For the Carolinas, the earliest examples of this literature are listed in William S. Powell, "Carolina in the Seventeenth Century: An Annotated Bibliography of Contemporary Publications," *North Carolina Historical Review*, 41

(1964): 74–104, and analyzed more fully in Hope Francis Kane, "Colonial Promotion and Promotion Literature of the Carolinas, 1660–1700," unpublished PhD. diss., Brown University, 1930. See also, Verner W. Crane, "The Promotion Literature of Colonial Georgia," in *Bibliographical Essays: A Tribute to Wilberforce Eames* (Cambridge, Mass., 1928).

7. The fullest biographical sketch of Nairne may be found in the introduction to Thomas Nairne, *Journalls to the Choctaws and Talapoosies* ed. Alexander Moore (University, Miss., 1988).

8. The call number of the manuscript is Codex Eng 10.

9. Transcripts of the Journals of the Society for the Propagation of the Gospel, Jan. 26, May 18, Aug. 17, 1711. Manuscripts Division, Library of Congress, Washington, D.C.

10. Nairne, *Letter*, 1; Norris, *Profitable Advice*, 1. Citations to both pamphlets are to the original pagination.

11. Nairne, *Letter*, 1, 3, 8, 51, 63.

12. *Profitable Advice*, 3, 5, 7, 69–71, 77, 100–102, 111–12.

13. Richard Blome, "A Description of Carolina," in *A Description of the Island of Jamaica* (London, 1672), 127; John Archdale, *A New Description of that Fertile and Pleasant Province of Carolina* (London, 1707), as reprinted in Alexander S. Salley, Jr., ed., *Narratives of Early Carolina 1650–1708* (New York, 1911), 308.

14. Blome, *Description*; Sir Robert Montgomery, *A Discourse Concerning the Design'd Establishment of a New Colony to the South of Carolina* (London, 1717), 18. Montgomery's work has been reprinted in a modern critical edition by J. Max Patrick, ed., *Azila: A Discourse by Sir Robert Montgomery, 1717, Projecting a Settlement in the Colony Later Known as Georgia* (Atlanta, 1948). This citation is to the Patrick edition. The appraisal of South Carolina's physical environment by contemporary writers is discussed cogently by H. Roy Merrens, "The Physical Environment of Early America: Images and Image Makers in Colonial South Carolina," *Geographical Review*, 59 (1969): 530–56.

15. Archdale, *New Description*, 290, 308; Robert Ferguson, *The Present State of Carolina with Advice to the Settlers* (London, 1682), 16, 18–19; Edward Randolph to the Board of Trade, Mar. 16, 1699, in Salley, ed., *Narratives of Early Carolina*, 209; Francis Le Jau to Philip Stubs, Apr. 15, 1707, in Frank J. Klingberg, ed., *The Carolina Chronicle of Dr. Francis Le Jau 1706–1717* (Berkeley and Los Angeles, 1956), 23–24; Thomas Ash, *Carolina; or a Description of the Present State of that Country* (London, 1682), as reprinted in Salley, ed., *Narratives of Early Carolina*, 138; Norris, *Profitable Advice*, 22; Nairne, *Letter*, 6; *Carolina Described More Fully Than Heretofore* (Dublin, 1684), 1–2; R[ichard] B[urton], *The English Empire in America* (London, 1685), 143.

16. Archdale, *New Description*, 290; "An Old Letter," [Mar. 1671], in W. Noel Sainsbury, et al., *Calendar of State Papers, Colonial Series*, 44 vols. (London, 1860–), *1669–71*, 186; Burton, *English Empire*, 143; John Stewart to William Dunlop, Apr. 27, 1690, in J. G. Dunlop and Mabel L. Webber, eds., "Letters from John Stewart to William Dunlop," *South Carolina Historical Magazine*, 32 (1931): 6.

17. *A True Description of Carolina* (London, [1682]), 1–2; Ferguson, *Present State*, 6–7, 9, 15, 27–28; Thomas to William Newe, May 17, 1682, in "Letters of Thomas Newe, 1682," in Salley, ed., *Narratives of Early Carolina*, 181; Maurice Mathews, "A Contemporary View of Carolina in 1680," *South Carolina Historical Magazine*, 55 (1954): 156–57; Norris, *Profitable Advice*, 21–23; Blome, *Description* 126–27, 129; Archdale, *New Description*, 288; Nairne, *Letter*, 7–8; Stewart to

Dunlop, Apr. 27, 1690, "Letters of Stewart," 4–5; Burton, *English Empire*, 137–42, 147; Peter Heylyn, *Cosmography in Foure Books* (London, 1713), 961.

18. On South Carolina's early development, see Peter H. Wood, *Black Majority: Negroes in Colonial South Carolina from 1676 through the Stono Rebellion* (New York, 1975), and Converse D. Clowse, *Economic Beginnings in Colonial South Carolina, 1670–1730* (Columbia, 1971).

19. Norris, *Profitable Advice*, 10.

20. Norris, *Profitable Advice*, 6–7, 61–62, 74, 107; Nairne, *Letter*, 3, 8, 42.

21. Nairne, *Letter*, 46–47; Norris, *Profitable Advice*, 13, 56.

22. Norris, *Profitable Advice*, 12–13, 23–24, 26–28, 39–40, 53, 61–62, 66, 86; Nairne, *Letter*, 7–13, 41, 50.

23. Norris, *Profitable Advice*, 96, 108.

24. Archdale, *New Description*, 290; Norris, *Profitable Advice*, 49, 92–96; Nairne, *Letter*, 52–54.

25. Nairne, *Letter*, 47, 51–56; Norris, *Profitable Advice*, 59–60, 92–96.

26. Norris, *Profitable Advice*, 46–48, 61, 76, 84.

27. Nairne, *Letter*, 54–55; Norris, *Profitable Advice*, 70, 96–99.

28. Nairne, *Letter*, 22–23, 30, 32–33, 38–39; Norris, *Profitable Advice*, 61.

29. Nairne, *Letter*, 38–39; Norris, *Profitable Advice*, 33–34, 61, 69, 90.

30. David Bertelson, *The Lazy South* (New York, 1967), 9–14; Norris, *Profitable Advice*, 100.

31. Nairne, *Letter*, 51; Norris, *Profitable Advice*, 17, 20, 31, 58, 61.

32. Norris, *Profitable Advice*, 55, 61–62; Nairne, *Letter*, 3, 56.

33. Nairne, *Letter*, 14–15; Norris, *Profitable Advice*, 21–22, 28, 63–65. On the high mortality in South Carolina, see H. Roy Merrens and George D. Terry, "Dying in Paradise: Malaria, Mortality, and the Perceptual Environment in Colonial South Carolina," *Journal of Southern History*, 50 (1984): 533–50.

34. M. Eugene Sirmans, *Colonial South Carolina: A Political History* (Chapel Hill, 1966), 44, 83–86, and Verner W. Crane, *The Southern Frontier 1670–1732* (Durham, 1928).

35. Nairne, *Letter*, 3–4, 31–34.

36. Nairne, *Letter*, 31–35.

37. See Joan Thirsk, *Economic Policy and Projects: The Development of a Consumer Society in Early Modern England* (Oxford, 1978), and Joyce Appleby, *Economic Thought and Ideology in Seventeenth-Century England* (Princeton, 1978).

38. Nairne, *Letter*, 8; Jack P. Greene, "Search for Identity: An Interpretation of Selected Patterns of Social Response in Eighteenth-Century America," *Journal of Social History*, 3 (1970): 189–224.

39. Norris, *Profitable Advice*, 16–18, 26, 30, 36–42, 44, 48, 50–51, 53–54, 68–69; Nairne, *Letter*, 43–44.

40. Norris, *Profitable Advice*, 13, 15, 39–42, 46, 62; Nairne, *Letter*, 25, 41, 44; Daniel Defoe, *Party Tyranny . . . in Carolina* (London, 1705), as reprinted in Salley, ed., *Narratives of Early Carolina*, 227.

41. Defoe, *Party Tyranny*, 227; Nairne, *Letter*, 8–9, 15–16, 41–46; Norris, *Profitable Advice*, 14, 34–35.

42. Nairne, *Letter*, 41–43, 45.

43. Norris, *Profitable Advice*, 32–33; Nairne, *Letter*, 17–27; Mathews, "A Contemporary View of Carolina," 154; Francis Le Jau to Secretary, Mar. 19, 1716, in Klingberg, ed., *Le Jau Chronicle*, 175.

44. Ferguson, *Present State*, 31, 34; Norris, *Profitable Advice*, 104.

45. Nairne, *Letter*, 3, 5, 26, 41, 56; Norris, *Profitable Advice*, 6–7, 11, 65, 85, 104.

46. Norris, *Profitable Advice*, 5–8, 73, 83, 104–105; Nairne, *Letter*, 56–63. Norris calculated the annual return for each laboring settler at £4, twenty percent less than Nairne.
47. Norris, *Profitable Advice*, 35–41, 72–96; Nairne, *Letter*, 10–11.
48. Nairne, *Letter*, 51–52; Norris, *Profitable Advice*, 85–90.
49. Nairne, *Letter*, 52–54; Norris, *Profitable Advice*, 92–96.
50. Nairne, *Letter*, 49–50, 55; Norris, *Profitable Advice*, 72–96.
51. Norris, *Profitable Advice*, 77, 96.

Pamphlet
One

A
LETTER

from

South Carolina;

Giving an
Account
of the

Soil, Air, Product, Trade,
Government, Laws, Religion, People,
Military Strength, &c. of that Province;

Together with the Manner and necessary
Charges of SETTLING a PLANTATION there,
and the *Annual Profit* it will produce

Written by a Swiss Gentleman, to his Friend at Bern

[THOMAS NAIRNE]

LONDON

Printed for *A. Baldwin,*
near the *Oxford-Arms* in *Warwick-lane.*   1710.

[3] SIR,

By the last Letters from you, which I had the Honour to receive, you was pleas'd to acquaint me with the Intention of some worthy Gentlemen of *Bern*, to settle a Fund for transporting annually a few Supernumeraries of our Nation, to the Province of *Carolina*; a Design both truly pious and generous, which at the same time consults the Interest of Religion, and the Civil Benefit of Mankind. How much better is it for those who have but a small Subsistence at home, to retire to a Place where they may with moderate Industry be supplied with all the Necessaries of Life, than to follow the miserable Trade of Destroying for a Shilling a Day? How much better for Men to improve their own Lands, for the Use of themselves, and Posterity; to sit under their own Vine, and eat the Fruits of their Labour; than to be instruments in the Hands of Tyrants, to ravage and depopulate the Earth, and that only to procure a poor Maintenance, and for [4] which there must hereafter be render'd a strict and severe Account?

Since I have been settled here, and for some time enjoyed the many Pleasures and Delights of a quiet peaceable Life, I have often reflected on the unhappy Condition of the Military Imployment, which I exchanged for this wherewith I am now blessed. What constant Troubles, Dangers and Fatigues attend it! How deplorable is it to behold the daily Ravages we are oblig'd to make! Who would not be mov'd with the Tears and Lamentations of the miserable? A free People, surrounded with potent Neighbours, must indeed and ought to be brave, and military, perfectly vers'd in Arms, either for their own Defence, or to assist their injur'd Allies. Nor is there any Name more great and noble than that of a Soldier; but then he must be one, who, like the Ancient Heroes, makes it his Business to destroy Monsters, assist the Impotent, redress Injuries; oppose Tyranny, and root out Oppression from the Face of the Earth. But to follow War meerly as a Trade, to hire one[']s self to the best Bidder, without Respect to the Merits of the Cause, is what I can never reconcile to the Principles either of revealed, or natural Religion: For this seems to be the perfect [5] Reverse of doing as we would be done by. And what shocks me most of all is, that some People devote their Children to the Wars before, or at least as soon as they are born. This seems to me rather worse, if possible, than the old heathenish Custom of sacrificing them to appease the Wrath of some angry God, for then the Mischief ended with the Lives of some few unfortunate Victims; but we sacrifice ours to a devouring Deity, who together with their own Deaths makes them the Occasion of that of many Innocents. And what renders these things more inexcusable is, that 'tis plain, Mankind is not reduc'd to the unhappy Necessity of Killing one another for Bread; since upon a due Calculation, the Earth is so far from being overstock'd with People, that 'tis capable of containing ten times the Number of its present Inhabitants. What vast and goodly Countries are there in the World, wholly, or for the most part unpeopled, and yet very capable of producing all things both for the Necessity and Conveniency of Life? An instance of which is this Province, whereof since you are pleas'd to desire some Account from me, I shall, without any Apology, proceed to obey your Commands, and in as small a compass as possible, give you a View of such [6] Things as are necessary to be known, by one who designs to settle there, to which I shall principally confine my Discourse.

Description.

Carolina is a Province of the *English America*, joining on the North-East to *Virginia*, between *36* and *29* Degrees North Latitude. It is divided into two Governments, commonly call'd *North* and *South Carolina. North Carolina* joins to *Virginia*, and that Part thereof now inhabited by the *English*, lies between *35* and *36* Degrees N. Latitude. The Parts of *South Carolina*, now possess'd by the English, lie between *32* and *33* Degrees N. Latitude, and about *60* Degrees Longitude, West from the Lands-End of *England*.

Between the same Parallels with *South Carolina*, lie some of the most fertile Countries in the World, as some Parts of the Coast of *Barbary*, all the middle Part of *China*, from the middle to the South Parts of *Japan*, those Countries of *India* about *Lahore*, the best part of *Persia*, *Egypt* and *Syria*.

Situation.

Carolina is in general a plain champain Country, having no considerable Hills for the Space of 1000 Miles together along the Coast, within 100 Miles of the Sea. There are, however, almost every where, Risings or gentle Ascents, from 5 Foot to 50, 60, or 70, [7] above the Level of the highest Tide.

Behind these vast champain Countries lies a high Ridge of Mountains, which beginning in the Lat[itude] of 34, 90 or 100 Miles to the Eastward of the *Missis[s]ippi*, run almost parallel with the Sea-coast, behind all *Florida*, both the *Carolinas, Virginia* and *Maryland*. The most common and usual Distance from the Foot of the Mountains to the Sea, is about 200 Miles. The Springs and Fountains of most of our great Rivers are in these Hills, which abound with innumerable Rivulets, and these meeting afterwards together, form many large Rivers; by the Course of which it appears, that the Land has a gradual, tho' insensible Descent from the Mountains to the Sea.

Trees.

This great Plain is one continued Forest, well stock'd with Oaks of several Kinds, Chestnut, Walnut, Hickery; several Kinds of Firr, Cypress of two Kinds, Cedar, Poplar, or the Tulip-tree, Laurel, Bay, Myrtle, Hasel, Beech, Ash, Elm, and Variety of others, whose Names are scarce known.

Fish.

The Sea-Coast is full of Islands, Sounds, Bays, Marshes, Rivers, and Creeks of Salt-Water, where the Tide useth to rise from 5 Foot to 7, seldom higher. These are well stor'd with great Variety of excellent Fish, the most common whereof are Bass, Drum, Whi[8]tings, Trouts, Herrings, Mullets, Rocks, Sturgeons, Shads,

Sheepsheads, Place, Flounders, Small Turtle, Crabs, Oisters, Muscles, Cockles, Shrimps, &c. Such Fish that are common and not eaten, are Whales, Grampoises, Porpoises, Sharks, Dog-fish, Garb, Stingrays, Saw-fish, Fidlers, and Periwincles.

This Province is capable of containing above 60 times the Number of its present Inhabitants; and there is no Place in the Continent of *America*, where People can transport themselves to greater Advantage.

South Carolina.

Now as *South Carolina* far excells the other in Improvements and navigable Rivers, I shall confine my Discourse to that, and acquaint you with its Product, Trade, Government, People, Laws, and lastly, with an Account of what is necessary to settle a Man comfortably there.

Product.

Besides the Things already mention'd, *South Carolina* naturally produces Black Mulberries, Walnuts, Chesnuts, Chincapines, which is a small Chesnut, and five or six Kinds of Acorns, all which the *Indians*, like the Primitive Race of Mankind, make Use of for Food; wild Potatoes, and several other eatable Roots, wild Plums, Variety of Grapes, Medlars, Huckle-berries, Strawberries, Hasel-nuts, Myrtle-berries, of which Wax is made; also Cedar-berries, Su[9]mach, Sassafras, China-Root, great and small Snake-root, with Variety of other Physical Roots and Herbs, and many Flowers, which spring up of themselves, and flourish in their Kind, every Season of the Year.

Many things have likewise been transplanted hither, which thrive very well with us, as White Mulberries, Grapes from the *Made[i]ras*, and elsewhere; all Kinds of *English* Garden-herbs, six or seven Sorts of Potatoes, all of them very good; *Indian* Corn three Sorts, *Indian* Pease five or six Kinds, *Indian* Beans several Kinds, Kidney-beans, *French* Beans, Pompions, Squashes, Gourds, Pomelons, Cucumbers, Musk-melons, Water-melons, Tobacco, Rice three or four Sorts, Oats, Rie, Barley, and some Wheat, tho' not much.

Fruits Planted.
Our Fruits are Apples, Pears, Quinces, Figs three or four Kinds,
Oranges, Pomegranates, Peaches fourteen or fifteen Sorts.

Tho' we have as great Variety of good Peaches as any Place,
perhaps, in the World, yet the principal Use made of them is to
feed Hogs, for which End, large Orchards are planted. The
Peach-trees with us are all Standards; they yield Fruit in three
Years from the Stone, the Fourth Year bear plentifully, and the
fifth are large spreading Trees.

[10] Most Kinds of *British* Fruits prosper best up in the
Country, at some Distance from Salt Water; but Figs, Peaches,
Pomegranates and the like, grow best nigh the Sea.

Seasons of Sowing.
Our Season of Sowing is from the First of *March* to the tenth of
June. The principal Seed-time of Rice, from the first of *April* to the
twentieth of *May;* of *Indian* Corn, Pease and Beans, the last Week
of *March,* all *April, May,* and the *first* ten Days of *June.* In *March*
and *April* we set Potatoes, Pompions, Cucumbers, Melons,
Kidney-beans, &c.

The usual Produce of an Acre of *Indian* Corn, is from *18* to *30*
Bushels, and *6* Bushels of *Indian* Pease, which run like a Vine
among the Corn: About a Gallon of *Indian* Corn sows an Acre.

Rice is sowed in Furrows, about 18 Inches distant, a Peck
usually sows an Acre, which yields seldom less than *30* Bushels,
or more than *60*, but betwixt these two, as the Land is either
better or worse.

Harvest.
Rice is reap'd in *September,* to the eighth of *October; Indian* Corn
and Pease from the first of *October* to the tenth of *November:*
Several Kinds of Pulse are ripe in *May* and *June.*

Ripe Fruits.
We have Pompions, Melons, Cucumbers, Squashes, and other
Vine-Fruits, which ripen, and are eat al[l] the [11] Summer, from
the middle of *June* to the first of *October.* Fig-trees bear two Crops
a Year, one ripe at the End of *June,* the other all *August.* By so

great variety of Peaches, Melocotons, and Nectarines, there is this Advantage, that we have them in Season from the 20th of *June* to the End of *September*, for during all that Time, one Kind or another of them is in Perfection.

Rice is clean'd by Mills, turned with Oxen or Horses. 'Tis very much sow'd here, not only because it is a vendible Commodity, but thriving best in low moist Lands, it inclines People to improve that Sort of Ground, which being planted a few Years with Rice, and then laid by, turns to the best Pasture.

Silk-worms.

Silk-worms with us are hatch'd from the Eggs about the 6th of *March*, Nature having wisely ordain'd them to enter into this new Form of Being, at the same time that the Mulberry-Leaves, which are their Food, begin to open. Being attended and fed six Weeks, they eat no more, but have small Bushes set up for them to spin themselves into Balls, which thrown into warm Water, are wound off into raw Silk.

Rosin.

Rosin, Tar and Pitch are all produc'd from the Pine-trees; Rosin, by cutting Channels in the standing green Trees, that meet in a Point at the Foot of the [12] Tree, where two or three small Pieces of Board are fitted to receive it. The Channels are cut as high as one can reach with an Axe, and the Bark is peeled off from all those Parts of the Tree that are expos'd to the Sun, that the Heat of it may the more easily force out the Turpentine, which falling upon the Boards placed at the Root, is gather'd and laid in Heaps, which melted in great Kettles, becomes Rosin.

Tar.

Tar is made thus: First they prepare a circular Floor of Clay, declining a little towards the Center, from which is laid a Pipe of Wood, whose upper Part is even with the Floor, and reaches 2 Foot without the Circumference; under this End the Earth is dug away, and Barrels placed to receive the Tar as it runs. Upon the Floor is built up a large Pile of Dry Pine-wood, split in Pieces, and surrounded with a Wall of Earth, which covers it all over, only a little at the Top, where the Fire is first kindled. After the Fire begins to burn, they cover that likewise with Earth, to the End there may be no Flame, but only Heat sufficient to force the Tar downward into the Floor. They temper the Heat as they please, by thrusting a Stick through the Earth, and letting the Air in at as many Places as they see convenient.

[13] *Pitch.*
Pitch is made either by boiling Tar in large Iron Kettles, set in Furnaces, or by burning it in round Clay-holes, made in the Earth.

Cattle.
Besides the various Sorts of Food produc'd by the Earth, *South Carolina* abounds with black Cattle, to a Degree much beyond any other *English* Colony; which is chiefly owing to the Mildness of the Winter, whereby the Planters are freed from the Trouble of providing for them, suffering them to feed all Winter in the Woods. These Creatures have mightily increas'd since the first settling of the Colony, about 40 Years ago. It was then reckon'd a great deal to have three or four Cows, but now some People have 1000 Head, but for one Man to have 200 is very common.

Hogs &c.
We have likewise Hogs in abundance, which go daily to feed in the Woods, and come home at Night; also some Sheep, and Goats.

Tame and Wild Fowl.
There are tame fowls of all sorts, and great variety of wild fowl, as turkeys, geese, ducks, wild pidgeons, partridges, brants, shel-drakes, teal; and near the sea, curlews, cranes, herons, snipes, pellicanes, gannets, sea-larks, and many others.

Wild Beasts.
The wild beasts, which the woods afford for game, are rabbets, foxes, racoons, possums, squirrels, wild cats, deer, [14] elks, buffaloes, bears, tygers, wild kine and hogs. Tho' the names of some of these creatures are frightful to those who never saw them, yet they are not so to us, for there is none of them, but will

fly from a man; nor do they any injury but to sheep, hogs, and young calves.

Air.

The Air of *Carolina* is generally very clear and fine, even when the greatest Rains fall, the Weather does not continue long cloudy, for the Sun soon dissipates the Fogs, and restores the Air to its usual Serenity. During the Heat of Summer, the Rains are very refreshing and agreeable, and the Thunder that accompanies them, tho' naturally terrifying, is welcome upon Account of its rarifying the Air. Earthquakes have never yet been known, or heard of in this Country.

Temperature of the Months.

The Heats of *Carolina* are indeed troublesome to Strangers in *June*, *July*, and *August*, in which Months are smart Claps of Thunder, tho' seldom doing any Prejudice. But the Inconveniency from the Heat during that Time, is made easie by shady Groves, open airy Rooms, Arbours, and Summer-houses; and to make some amends for it, no Country can afford pleasanter Weather, in the Spring, Fall, and greatest Part of Winter. *September, October, November*, are pleasant dry Months, neither hot [15] nor cold. *December* and *January* are moderately cold, sometimes accompanied with sharp cold North-West Winds, and Frost, which seldom last above two or three Days at a Time. There is scarce ever any Snow, or if it does fall, it lies not above one Night. *February* and *March* are pleasant, fair, dry Months, answering in Temperature to *April* and *May* in *England*, which with us are very agreeable Months, the Weather being then clear and fair, refreshed with gentle Showers once in eight or ten Days, but equal in Heat in *June* and *July* in *England*.

Trade.

The Trade between *South Carolina* and *Great Britain*, does, one Year with another, employ 22 Sail of Ships, laden hither with all Sorts of Woollen Cloaths, Stuffs, and Druggets, Linnens, Hollands, printed Linnen and Callicoe, Silks and Muslins, Nails of all sizes, Hoes, Hatchets, and all Kinds of Iron-ware, Bed-ticks, strong Beer, bottled Syder, Raisins, fine Earthen-ware, Pipes,

Paper, Rugs, Blankets, Quilts, Hats from 2 s. to 12 s. Price, Stockings from 1 s. to 8 s. Price, Gloves, Pewter Dishes and Plates, Brass and Copper Ware, Guns, Powder, Bullets, Flints, Glass Beads, Cordage, Woollen and Cotten Cards, Steel Hand-mills, Grind-stones, Looking and Drinking Glasses, Lace, Thread [16] course and fine, Mohair, and all Kinds of Trimming for Cloaths, Pins, Needles, &c. In return for which are remitted from hence about seventy Thousand Deer-skins a Year, some Furs, Rosin, Tar, Raw Silk, Rice, and formerly Indigo. But since all these don't balance the continual Demand of *European* Goods, and Negro Slaves, sent us by the *English* Merchants, there is likewise sent to *England*, some Cocoa-nuts, Sugar, Tortoise-shell, Money, and other Things, which we have from the *American* Islands, in return for our Provisions. Besides the 22 Sail above-mention'd, there enter and clear annually at the Port of *Charlestown*, about *60* Sail of Ships, Sloops, and Brigantines, all from some Places of *Africa* or *America*.

From *Jamaica*, *St. Thomas's*, *Currasso*, *Barbadoes*, and the *Le[e]ward Islands*, we have Sugar, Rum, Molosses, Cotton, Choco-late made up, Coco-nuts, Negroes, and Mon[e]y. In return whereof we send Beef, Pork, Butter, Candles, Soap, Tallow, Myrtle-wax Candles, Rice, some Pitch and Tar, Cedar and Pine-boards, Shingles, Hoop-staves, and Heads for Barrels.

From *New-England*, *New York*, and *Pen[n]sylvania*, we have Wheat-flower, Bisket, strong Beer, Cyder, salt Fish, Onions, Apples, Hops; and return [17] them ta[n]n'd Hides, small Deer-skins, Gloves, Rice, Slaves taken by the *Indians* in War, some Tar and Pitch.

From *Made[i]ra* and the Western Islands, we have Wine, and in return, supply them with Provisions, Staves, and Heads for Barrels, &c. Our Salt comes from the *Bahama* Islands.

From *Guinea*, and other Parts of the Coast of *Africa*, are imported Negroe-Slaves; but the Ships that bring them being sent, with the Effects to purchase them, from *England*, the Returns are sent thither.

Government.

In vain would all the Advantages of a fine Air, fruitful Soil, and good Trade, be to us, if not incouraged to improve them by a good Government and Laws. Even your Mountains are preferable to *Lombardy* itself, if one must there be subject to the Caprice and absolute Pleasure of a *French* Intendant. But this Colony was founded upon the generous Principles of civil and religious Liberty, on which noble Foundation it hath been raised to its present Height. And because it is a received Maxim, That all Things prosper best by the Use of the same Means, whereby they were first formed, the People have not been wanting to secure these valuable Priviledges, the Assemblies, from time to time, having passed Laws [18] to transmit these Blessings to Posterity, as fully and largely as we enjoy them at present; so that the civil Rights of *Englishmen*, together with a just, impartial, and intire Liberty of Conscience, are as firmly secured to the Inhabitants of this Province, as Acts of the general Assembly can make them.

The Known Laws among us are the Measure and Bounds of Power. The highest in Authority cannot legally oppress or insult the meanest. Fines, Imprisonments, Death, or other Punishments, are not left to the arbitrary Decisions of the Governours and Judges, but are nicely and particularly prescribed by the Laws. Those who are intrusted with the Executive Part of the Government, are obliged to know their bounds, so far they may go and no farther. It is not here as in those Countries where Slavery is fixed, and strug[g]ling with the Chains rivets them the faster. But Liberty is so well and legally established, that whatever Mismanagements may be occasion'd from those who have the Administration, while a Sense of Freedom remains, the Vigour of the Constitution will throw off these politick Diseases, and restore the Publick to a State of Health.

The Foundation of this Government is a Charter granted by King *Charles* II. [19] to eight Proprietors, which, together with a Title to the Land, gives them ample Priviledges and Jurisdictions, particularly all such as are any way necessary, to the forming or well ordering a Body politick; reserving always an Allegiance to the Crown of *England*, and to the People who shall settle in *Carolina*, all Rights, Liberties and Franchises of *Englishmen*. By which express Limitation in behalf of his Subjects, the King put it out of their Lordships['] Power to lay any Hardships upon them, contrary to the Laws of *England*.[1]

This Province is at present in the Hands of the Right

Honourable *William* Lord *Craven*, Palatine, the Most Noble *Henry* Duke of *Beaufort*, the Right Honourable Lord *Carteret*, Sir *John Colleton, Maurice Ashl[e]y* Esq, Mr. *John Danson* and Mr. *Blake*, a Minor.[2] The Power of the Palatine is considerable, for he hath a Negative in all Orders or Decisions of the whole Board; neither can the other Proprietors hold a Board without he be present, or one delegated to act for him. He cannot, however, enact any thing without the Concurrence of four Proprietors, besides himself.[3] The same Place that the Palatine hath at the Board of Proprietors in *England*, the Governour hath in *Carolina*, besides the Power granted him by Commission.

[20] *Governour and Council.*
The Governour calls and presides in all Councils of State, which consist of the eight Proprietor's Deputies. With the Assent of four Deputies, he calls, prorogues, or dissolves, the general Assemblies; appoints Civil Officers, such as Justices of the Peace. He assents to, or dissents from Laws, hath a negative Voice in all Acts, Orders, or Ordinances of the general Assemblies; he alone commissionates all military Officers, and disposes of the Militia according to Law, for Defence of the Colony. He bears the Title of Governour, Captain-General, and Admiral, of *South* and *North Carolina*.

In all Affairs, except those that are military, every Counsellour hath an equal Vote with the Governour, and he can do nothing without the Concurrence of four of them at least.

While the Parliament sits, the Governour, with the other seven Deputies, make the upper House, in the Intervals of Parliament, they are the Council of State and Court of Chancery.

The Governour of *South Carolina* is appointed by Commission, sign'd by the Palatine, and at least four more of the Lords Proprietors, during Pleasure. Each Member of the Council hath a Deputation from one or other of the Proprietors, whom he represents. Upon [21] the Death or Resignation of any Member of the Council, the Vacancy is filled by the Votes of the Majority of those who remain: And upon the Death of any Governour, one of the Proprietor[']s Deputies is elected Governour by the rest, and continues so till their Lordships send another from *England*, or a new Commission to some other Person.

General Assemblies.

The Form of Government is as nigh as conveniently can be to that of *England*. The Legislature consists of two Chambers, the upper, which is compos'd of the eight Proprietor[']s Deputies; and the lower of thirty Representatives, chosen by the People. By Law, the Governour is obliged to call an Assembly every two Years.[4]

The general Assemblies are call'd by Writs, issued out of the Secretarie[']s Office, under the Seal of the Colony, and Test of the Governour: These are directed to the Sheriff of each County, bearing Date forty Days before the Return, and he is to take Care that they be duly published.

The first Business of the Commons is to choose a Speaker, which being done, they present him to the Governour in a full House, who approves him; then they return to their own House, and proceed to do business, choosing Committees, and in all other Respects imitating the [22] House of Commons in *England*, as nigh as possible.

The lower House seldom passes Imposition-Acts for any time above two Years; and the Reason is, That themselves may be always necessary, and retain that Power they have by Law, and preserve the just Ballance of the Government: They likewise claim all the Powers, Priviledges, and Immunities, which the House of Commons have in *Great Britain*.

They appoint the publick Treasurer, call him to an Account, and dismiss him, when they see fit, by a Vote of their House. For 'tis a received opinion among them, that the Power of appointing, examining, censuring, and displacing those who have the public Money in their Hands, is much better lodg'd in the House of Commons, who have so great an Interest in the Colony, than in the Hands of any Governour, for Reasons generally known in *America*.

The lower House likewise presents to the Governour all Persons, who are to receive his Commissions, and have any Salary out of the publick Treasury, such as Captains of Forts, and the like. The Governour, it is true, hath the Power of granting Commissions to these and other Officers, but then the Treasurer [23] cannot pay them any Salary, unless they have been first recommended by the House of Commons.[5]

All Bills generally begin, and are form'd in the House of

Commons, but no Act, Order, or Ordinance, is of any Force, without having passed both Houses in due Parliamentary Form. All Bills are read three several Times on three several Days, in each House, before they can pass into a Law.

The Method of ratifying Laws is this; After a Bill or Bills have passed both Houses, in due Form, the Clerk of the lower House is order'd to engross them, upon fair Paper or Vellum. The Speaker, with the whole House, attend the Governour in the upper House, and present the Bills; then the Governour reads the Title, signs and seals the bill, and says, *In the Name of his Excellency*, William *Lord* Craven, *Palatine, I Ratifie and Confirm this Law*. Every one of the other Deputies do and say the like, each in the Name of his Principal. After a Bill is thus ratified, sign'd and seal'd by the Governour and four Deputies, it is then proclaim'd and held for Law.

Neither the Members of the Council, nor the House of Commons, in this Province, have any Allowance for attending the publick Service, but do it at their own Expences.

[24] *Laws.*
The Laws of South Carolina are either Acts of our own general Assemblies, or the Statute or Common Law of *England*. It is taken for granted with us, that no *English* Laws bind the Plantations, except such as particularly mention them, till they are put in Force by Act of Assembly, in each particular Province. Because Promulgation is in a manner absolutely necessary to render any Law obligatory, the general Assembly first peruse all *English* Acts of Parliament, draw up an Account of as many intire ones, and Parts of others, as are fit for this Province, and by an Act of Assembly mentioning these Acts, they put them in Force. Thus we have Schedules of such *English* Acts of Parliament made Law, beginning with the great Charter of *England*, and running thro' all the Statutes, down to those made in the Reign of her present Majesty. And this is held to be the most rational Method, both for distinguishing such *English* Laws as are not proper for this Colony, and for promulgating them that are.

By an Act of Assembly, the Common Law of *England* is ordain'd to be of Force here, in Cases not provided for by the Statutes of this Province; with this Exception, nevertheless, that

[25] nothing of a Religious or Ecclesiastical Nature, tho' practised in *England*, by the Common Law, shall be of any Force in *South Carolina*.[6]

Habeas Corpus.

By the Laws of this Colony, the Governour alone, the Chief Justice alone, any two of the Council, or two Justices of the Peace, have the same Power of granting Writs of *Habeas Corpus*, as the Justices of either Bench have in *England*, and are under the same Penalties in case of Neglect or Refusal.[7]

Method of Summoning Juries.

Tho' it is Commendation sufficient for our Laws, to say they are as nigh to those of *England*, as conveniently may be, yet we have in several things refin'd upon the *English* Laws. For Instance: The Jurors are not here return'd by the Sheriffs, but the Names of all the best qualified Persons in the County are agreed upon and settled by Act of Assembly, and put together into a Ballot-box. At the End of every Court this is set upon the Table, before the Judge and Bench, and after it is shaken, a little Child draws out 48 Names, which are read, and a List of them taken by the Sheriff, that he may know whom to summons. These 48 are put in the second Division of the Ballot-box, out of which, at the opening of the next Court, another Child draws 12, who are to serve as Jurors, and if any just [26] Exception be made, he draws others, until the Jury be full. The same Method, with little Alteration, is taken in returning Juries for the Sessions of the Peace. The Names of those who have served are put in the third Division of the Box, where they lie till those in the first Division are almost all drawn, and then they are again put into this. The Reason of their lying in the third Division is, because one Set of Persons should not be too much burthen'd, but that all should have an equal Share of the Trouble, as nigh as may be.

The Ballot-box hath three Locks and Keys, kept by three several Persons appointed by the general Assembly, whereof the Judge of the Court is one; neither can the Box be opened without the Presence of those three.[8]

The Reason of all this Precaution in returning Jurors is, for the better and more effectual Preservation of the Lives and Estates of the Inhabitants. For the Sheriffs, Marshals, and all other such Officers, being appointed by the Governour, and keeping their Places only during his Pleasure, if the returning of Juries lay in their Power, 'tis more than probable, they might at some time or other, pack such Instruments as would be ready to gratify him, to the Ruin of any Person against who he had con[27]ceiv'd Malice or Displeasure. Considering therefore, how easily frivolous and unjust Prosecutions are set on foot, and Evidences fit for any Turn may be procur'd, nothing can be a greater Security than this noble Law; for after all the Arts and Management betwixt a bad Governour, Judge, and Attorney General, to carry on an illegal Prosecution, the whole Contrivance is at last spoiled by the Impossibility of Packing a Jury for the Purpose.

Our Legislators have wisely consider'd the Frailty and Passions of Men, how difficult it is for those in Power to keep themselves within Bounds, and how inclin'd they are to Resentment; for which Reason, tho' they never endeavoured to abridge their Governour's Power of doing Good, yet, by this and other Methods, they have aimed at leaving them as few Opportunities of doing Hurt as is possible.

Courts of Justice.
For Administration of Justice, Courts of Common-Pleas are held quarterly, by a Chief Justice and some Assistants. No Cause less than forty Shillings can be brought before this Court; all under that Sum are determin'd in an expeditious Manner, by a Justice of the Peace.[9]

There is no other Court superiour to this but the Chancery, of which the Governour is Chief Judge, and the o[28]ther Counsellours his Assistants. All Appeals from the Common-Pleas are finally determin'd in Chancery, and from thence are issued out Exhibitions and Supersedeas's to inferiour Courts. They act in that Court after the same Manner, and claim the same Power, which the Court of Chancery hath in *England*.[10]

Sessions for Pleas of the Crown.
The same Judge and Assistants, who keep the Court of Common-Pleas, do, every six Months, hold a Sessions of the Peace, and general Goal[sic]-Delivery for the whole Province; before whom

are tried all Pleas of the Crown. They sit generally three or four Days at a Time, till all Business be done. This Court is attended with all its proper Officers, as the Queen's Attorney, Constables, Marshal, Goaler[sic], &c. [11]

The Governour signs the Warrant for Execution of Criminals, and hath Power, if he please, to grant a Reprieve, till their Lordships either pardon them, or signifie their Pleasure to the contrary.

Special Courts.

For the Benefit of Merchants and others, who are going out of the Province, and cannot stay the common Methods of Proceeding at the ordinary Courts, upon Application made to the Chief Justice, he is by Law oblig'd immediately to call a Special Court, to determine their Affairs; so that Strangers [29] have no just Cause given of complaining, that the Laws of this Colony have not made suitable Provision in their behalf.

Probat[e]s of Wills.

Probat[e]s of Wills, and Letters of Administration, are granted by the Governour in Council, who is reckoned the Ordinary of the Place, and gives Marriage-Licences, which are left ready sign'd, with a Blank for the Names, in the Secretary's Office: But those who take them out, generally enter into Bonds, with sufficient Securities, that they have no Wife already, and that their intended Marriage is in all Respects legal. [12]

All Writs and Precepts run in the Name of his Excellency the Palatine, and the rest of the true and absolute Lords Proprietors of *Carolina*. The Attorneys are licensed by the Chief Justice.

The Chief Justice's Commission is from the Lords Proprietors, and is usually during Pleasure.

Officers.

Besides the Governour and Chief Justice, the Lords Proprietors appoint the Receiver of their Revenues, Surveyour General, Naval Officer, &c.

The Secretary's Business is to keep the publick Records of the Country, to take care that they be fairly laid up, to make and record all Patents for Land, to file the Certificates of Surveys, to keep a Register of all Deeds, Conveyances, Probat[e]s of Wills, and Letters of [30] Administration, to write Commissions for Officers civil and military.

The Receiver of the Lords Proprietors has the Charge of their Lordships['] Revenue, receives the Mon[e]y paid for the Sale, and Rents of Lands, all Fines in criminal Cases, and Escheats; out of which he pays Salaries to the Governour, Chief Justice, Queen's Attorney, and other incident Charges relating to the Support of the Government.

Publick Revenues.

The Treasurer for the Country is appointed by the House of Commons. He keeps all the publick Accounts, receives all Taxes, Duties, and Imposts, appointed by Acts of Assembly; out of which he pays all Sums of Mon[e]y, ordain'd to be paid by any Law of the Province, or any Order or Ordinance of Parliament, sign'd by the Governour and Speaker of the House of Commons. Once, during every Session of the Assembly, a Committee of the House of Commons is appointed to examine his Accounts, who generally make a strict Enquiry, compare every Article with his Vouchers, and then make Report of the whole to the House, who, if there be no just Objection, pass the Accounts, order them to be sign'd by the Speaker, and that is his *Quietus*. This frequent Examination of the publick Revenues and Disbursements, keeps us from being embarrass'd with tedious and intricate Accounts.

[31] Military Strength and Discipline.

For Defence of the Colony, our Laws oblige every Male Person from 16 to 60 Years of Age, to bear Arms, who are all under their proper Captains, Majors, and Colonels, by whom they are duly exercis'd once in two Months.[13] It is not here as in *England*, where an ordinary Mechanic thinks himself too good to be a Soldier. Every one among us is versed in Arms, from the Governour to the meanest Servant, and are all so far from thinking it below them, that most People take Delight in military Affairs, and think no body so fit to defend their Properties as themselves. We have the same Opinion of Arms as the *Romans*, and other free People, generally had, and believe them to be best intrusted with those who have the greatest Interest.

There are likewise enrolled in our Militia, a considerable Number of active, able, Negro Slaves; and the Law gives every one of those his Freedom, who in the Time of an Invasion, kills an Enemy; the Publick making Satisfaction to his Master for the Damage sustained by the Slaves's Manumission.[14]

Besides these Forces, *English* Officers are appointed over the *Indians* with whom we are in Friendship, who are order'd, with the utmost Expedition, to [32] draw them down to the Sea-coast, upon the first News of an Allarm. This is reckon'd a very considerable Part of our Strength, for there being some thousands of these, who are hardy, active, and good Marksmen, excellent at an Ambuscade, and who are brought together with little or no Charge; in all Probability, if the *French* or *Spaniards* should make any Attempt upon *Carolina*, they might have Reason to repent it.

Arms.

The Arms which every one is obliged to have, and bring into the Field, are a good Fusee, carrying a Bullet of about 18 to the Pound, a Cartridge-box, so waxt as to keep out all Water, with at least 16 Cartridges, a Sword, or Cutlass, Worm, Picker, spare Flints, &c.

The Inhabitants of *Carolina*, especially those born there, are dextrous and expert in the Use of Fire-Arms. If regular Troops excel[l] in performing the Postures, this Militia is much superiour in making a true Shot. The Habit of Shooting so very well is acquir'd by the frequent Pursuit of Game in the Forests.

We have no regular Troops in *Carolina*, except a very few in the Fort, and Sentinels in several Places along the Coast. Upon any Allarm, there are proper Officers appointed to lead a cer[33]tain Body of Militia into those Forts where they may be most useful. And as we have no regular Troops, for many Reasons we desire none. A Planter who keeps his Body fit for Service, by Action and a regular Life, is doubtless a better Soldier, upon Occasion, than a Company of raw Fellows raised in *England*, whose Spirits and Vigour are soon pall'd by an idle, effeminate Life, in a warm Climate. And the same Charges that would transport two or three Companies of regular Troops hither, to serve as Soldiers, would send the same Number of

Men, and enable them to settle as Planters, who, by their Industry, would add to the Improvement and Trade of the Province, and be equally serviceable for its Defence.

Forts.

Since the Beginning of this War[15] we have exerted our selves very much in Defence of the Colony, having fortified *Charlestown* with strong and regular Works, and erected another Fort upon a Point of Land, at the Mouth of *Ashly* River, which commands the Channel so well, that Ships can't easily pass it, when compleatly finished, and furnished with large Guns. We have likewise been at great Expences in providing necessary Supplies of Arms and Ammunition.

Besides this, there have been undertaken several foreign Expeditions; one a[34]gainst St. *Augustine*,[16] a Town and Garrison of the *Spaniards*, on the Coast of *Florida*, in the Latitude of 29 Degrees; and others against the *Spaniards* and *Indians* of *Apalachia*.[17] I shall not trouble you with a long Account of these Enterprises, but only tell you our Forces intirely broke and ruin'd the Strength of the *Spaniards* in *Florida*, destroy'd the whole Country, burnt the Towns, brought all the *Indians*, who were not kill'd or made Slaves, into our own Territories, so that there remains not now, so much as one Village with ten Houses in it, in all *Florida*, that is subject to the *Spaniards*; nor have they any Houses or Cattle left, but such as they can protect by the Guns of their Castle of St. *Augustine*, that alone being now in their Hands, and which is continually infested by the perpetual Incursions of the *Indians*, subject to this Province.

These Expeditions have added very much to our Strength and Safety; First, by reducing the *Spanish* Power in *Florida* so low, that they are altogether uncapable of ever hurting us; then by training our *Indian* Subjects in the Use of Arms, and Knowledge of War, which would be of great Service to us, in case of any Invasion from an Enemy; and, what is yet more considerable, by drawing over to our Side, or destroying, all the *Indians*, [35] within 700 Miles of *Charlestown*. This makes it impracticable for any *European* Nation to settle on that Coast, otherwise than as Subjects to the Crown of *Great Britain*; because we are capable of giving them such continual Molestation, by the Incursions of our Savages, that they could not easily subsist, or venture to make any Improvement.

Exchequer Bills and Public Credit.

The Charges of these Fortifications and Expeditions, though very necessary, were yet so considerable, that they created some Uneasiness, and the Assembly finding it was in vain to struggle with the Difficulty, by raising annual Taxes, which could not have been levied soon enough to answer the present Exigency, they concluded to stamp Bills of Credit, at first for about 6000 Pounds, and having had Experience of them, about 10000 Pounds more since.

By the Laws that establish the Bills of Credit, their Currency is secur'd. To proffer any Payment with them is a Tender in Law, so that if the Creditor refuse to take them, he loseth his Money, and the Debtor is discharg'd from the Minute of the Refusal. But we have no Instance of that Kind, the Funds upon which they are made being so good, that they pass in all Payments without any Demur or Dissatisfaction.[18]

[36] The House of Commons took extraordinary Care that the Credit of these public Bills should be well establish'd. They suffer'd none to be made by private Banks, not being willing to put it in their Power to injure the Public; but fix'd them on such Foundations which nothing could destroy, but what, at the same Time, should ruin the whole Province; that is, upon Acts of Assembly, appointing such Duties as were not to be taken off till the Bills of Credit were entirely cancell'd.

There never was yet found among us one Instance of counterfeiting these Bills, and all the Care imaginable has been taken to prevent it: For being first stamp'd with Blanks left for the Sums, they were brought into a Chamber adjoining to the House of Commons, where they were fill'd up, by a Committee of five, two Members of the Council, and three of the lower House, who, besides the Flourish and the Counter-part, usual in *England*, sign'd them with their Hands, and seal'd them with one common Seal; so that whoever attempted to counterfeit, must, besides the indenting and intricate Flourish, imitate five several well known

Hands, and a Seal, which could not remain long undiscover'd, since all these Bills are continually circulating thro' the Treasury.

[37] After the Bills were numb[e]red, indented, sign'd and seal'd, they were given to the Treasurer, together with a Schedule of all Debts due from the Public, which he immediately discharg'd with them. Three Commissioners are appointed by the Assembly to examine the Treasurer's Books weekly, and to see that such Bills, lying in his Hands, be cancell'd, which the necessary Expences of the Public do not require to be used.

Our Bills of Credit were at first made to run with 12 *per Cent.* Interest; but upon making the second Parcel, the Assembly was sensible of the great Inconvenience of that Method. For it not only made the Currency more difficult, by reason of the Endorsements, and computing the Times they had lain in the Treasury; but gave the Treasurer likewise an Opportunity of injuring the Public, by giving Credit for what Time he thought fit, as often as they came into his Hands. Besides, the Interest gave Encouragement to People to hoard them, which was a common Prejudice, by Keeping so great a Part of the Cash from circulating in Trade. And Lastly, this devouring Interest was such a constant Addition to the public Debt, that, if continued, it would have made it impossible to sink the Bills in any reasonable Time, unless by troublesome Taxes.

[38] These Reasons made the Assembly Enact, That from that Time forward, the Bills of Credit should run to all intents and Purposes as they had done, without any Interest at all.[19] And we quickly found the Benefit of it. For this both eased the Public of a great Burthen, and the Bills circulated more in Trade, and with less Difficulty among the Common People. The Assembly indeed, by this Act, expos'd themselves to the Censure of those who little regard the public so long as their own private Interest is advanc'd; but they wisely consider'd, that to save the Public 2000 Pounds a Year was more to be regarded, than to gratifie the unreasonable Avarice of some particular Persons.

It is probable, there are very few Countries where public Credit is better preserved than with us, or where Paper-Cash circulates more smoothly. And this proceeds from every one[']s being satisfied of the Goodness of the Funds, and the Honour which the Assemblies have always taken Care to preserve, in discharging all just Demands upon the Public, together with the good Husbandry they have us'd in disposing of the Public Money; Frugality being a Vertue very useful in large Governments, but absolutely necessary in small and poor ones.

[39] Bills of Credit with us have never fallen lower than the intrinsic, nor can they well do so, upon those Principles whereon they are established.

Public Revenues.
There are at present no Taxes in *South Carolina*, either upon real or personal Estates: But the public Revenue arises from Duties laid upon all Spirits, Wines, and other Liquors; upon Slaves, Sugars, Molosses, Flower, Bisket, &c.[,] upon all dry Goods imported, 3 *l. per Cent.* and 3 *d. per* Skin upon all Dear-skins exported.[20] All these Duties together, may, at present, amount to about 4500 Pounds *per Ann[um]* out of which the yearly Disbursements are as follow.

To 10 Ministers of the Church of *England*	1000 *l.*
For finishing and repairing Fortifications	1000
For the Officers of Forts and Sentinels	600
To the Governour	200
For military Stores	300
Accidental Charges	400
	3500 *l.*

Which taken out of 4500 *l.* there remain yearly 1000 *l.* to cancel so many of the Bills of Credit.

This Computation is nigh the Truth this present Year; but the State of things is alterable, either by unexpected Demands upon the Public, or by the Increase of Trade, and consequently of the Revenue.

[40] Asses[s]ments.
Asses[s]ments have seldom been us'd with us: When there are any, the Method is, for the Assembly to ascertain the Sum to be raised, and appoint Assessors, who shall lay it equally upon all

real and personal Estates, throughout the Province. They appoint likewise Officers in every Precinct, who return to the Assessors, upon Oath, a Schedule both of the Persons and Estates, in their respective Divisions. All Persons who are assess'd have this Priviledge, That if they believe themselves tax'd for more than their due Proportion, they may swear to the real Value of their Estates, and so procure an Abatement of what they are over-rated.

Coin.

Besides Bills of Credit, the Money most common in this Province is *French* Pistoles, *Spanish* and *Arabian* Gold; which before the late Act, that regulates the Currency of Money in the *English* Colonies,[21] past at 6 *s.* and 3 *d.* a Penny-weight, and 3 *d.* every odd Grain; *Dutch* and *German* Dollars, and *Peruvian* Pieces of Eight, passed at 5 *s.*[,] *Mexican* Pieces of Eight, of twelve Penny-weight, at 5 *s.* every Penny-weight above twelve to seventeen being 3 1/2 *d.* more. We have likewise 7 1/2 *d.* and 3 1/2 *d.* Pieces of *Spanish* Money, commonly call'd Royals, and Half-Royals. There is little *English* Money, but what is, goes at 50 *1. per* [41] *Cent.* Advance, that is, a Crown at 7 *s.* and 6 *d.* a Guinea at 32 *s.* and 3 *d.* and so in proportion.

People.

South Carolina was first settled about the Year 1667. The Penal Laws then in Force in *Great Britain,* contributing very considerably to send the first *English* colonies hither. It has likewise had a large Addition of Inhabitants by the Revocation of the Edict of *Nants,* the *French* Refugees having found here a safe and pleasant Retreat, from the rigid Church Discipline of their Dragooning Apostles. They live in good Friendship with, and are belov'd by the *English,* who being sensible, that their Assistance has contributed not a little to improve the Country, have been ready to oblige them upon all Occasions, wherein it lay in their Power; as in passing general Laws of Naturalization, admitting them into all Posts Civil and Military.[22] And this good Understanding not only continues, but increases daily, by Cohabitation and Intermarriages.

The *European* Inhabitants of this Province are, for the most part, People of Sobriety and Industry; which, together with the Advantage of the Climate, enable them to live in great Affluence of most things necessary for Life. I may venture to say, that this Country is much better improv'd than any other *English* [42] Colony on the Continent of *America*, in proportion to the Length of Time, and Stock of *English* Mon[e]y originally expended in Settling it.

No People are more hospitable, generous, and willing to do good Offices to Strangers; every one is ready to entertain them freely, with the best they have. That Moroseness and Sullenness of Temper, so common in other Places, is very rare among us.

Tho' we are so happily situated, that no body is obliged to beg or want Food, yet the Charity of the Inhabitants is very remarkable, in taking suitable Methods to prevent any Persons falling into extream Necessity. For Commissioners are appointed by Act of Assembly, to take Care of the Poor, and necessary Helps are settled for that End; tho' there are few Occasions to make use of this Provision, unless towards the Widows or Children of such Strangers, who die before they are comfortably settled.[23] And even in these Cases so many People are inclined to support them, that the Commissioners are not often troubled; their Neighbours of Substance generally taking one or two such unfortunate Orphans, whom they not only educate, and provide for, with a great deal of Humanity, during their Minority, but likewise are very generous and liberal in assisting [43] them, after they are grown up, to settle themselves in the World. For People here are not arrived to that sordid Temper and partial Fondness, to breed their own Children to the Height of Delicacy, and suffer others of the same Blood and Nation, to be destitute of the common Necessaries of Life.

Those born of *European* Parents, are for the most part very temperate, and have generally an Aversion to excessive Drinking. I cannot at present call to mind above two or three in the whole Province, addicted to that Vice. They are likewise ingenious, of good Capacities, and quick Apprehensions, and have Heads excellently well turn'd for mechanical Works and Inventions; with little or no teaching, they'll make Houses, Mills, Sloops, Boats, and the like.

All People in this Colony are either Planters, Traders, Artisans, *Indian* Subjects, or Negroe Slaves. A Planter is a common Denomination for those who live by their own and their Servants['] Industry, improve their Estates, follow Tillage or Grasing, and make those Commodities which are transported from hence to *Great Britain,* and other Places.

It is not necessary to insert the exact Numbers of the several Inhabitants; but the Proportions they bear to one a[44]nother, and each to the whole, are as follows,

Whites { Planters, Traders, Artisans } as { 8 1/2, 1 1/2, 2 } to 12.

All the Whites, *Indian* Subjects, Negro Slaves to the whole, as { 12, 66, 22 } to 100

Servants.
There are very few *European* Servants, and these are treated with as much Gentleness as any where in the World, being seldom put to other Employments than to exercise some Trade, oversee a Plantation, or to carry Goods to Market; the greatest Drudgeries being perform'd by Slaves. And upon the Expiration of four Years, they who came Servants, are as free in all Respects, and as much entituled to the Privileges of the Country, as any other Inhabitants whatsoever.

Laws of Naturalization.
By many Acts of the General Assembly, all foreign Protestants, of what Denomination soever, are made Denizens within three Months after their Arrival, and no other Qualification requir'd than to go before some Magistrate, and take the Oath of Allegiance, by which the Person is naturalized to all Intents and Purposes.[24]

[45] Religion.
It must needs be very acceptable to all good Christians, to hear that Religion and Piety have increas'd and flourished among us,

in good Measure; the Labours of some reverend Persons, who have exerted themselves in the Service of their great Master, having been bless'd with very desireable Success; which besides the Advantages in respect to a future Life, has also greatly contributed to the Good of the Society, by refining those Dispositions which were otherwise rude and untractable.

There are eight Ministers of the Church of *England*, three *French* Protestant Congregations, whereof two of their Ministers are lately proselyted to the Church, five of *British* Presbyterians, one of Anabaptists, and a small one of Quakers. The Ministers of the Church of *England* have each 100 *l. per Annum,* paid out of the public Treasury, besides Contributions and Perquisites from their Parishioners. The other Ministers are maintain'd by voluntary Subscriptions. The Proportions that the several Parties in Religion do bear to the whole, and each other, is at present as follows,

[46] Episcopal Party			4 1/4	
Presbyterians, including those *French* who retain their own Discipline	to the		4 1/2	to 10
Anabaptists	whole,		1	
Quakers	as		0 1/4	
			10	

Lands.

Nothing can be more reasonable than the Price of Lands in this Province; we must do their Lordships the Justice to say, they have always, in that Respect, dealt with great Favour and Gentleness. The first twenty Years they got little or nothing at all, and since not much more than is barely sufficient to support the necessary Charges of the Government. By this Conduct the Proprietors have advanc'd the Interest of the *English* Nation to their own present Loss. For if their Lordships had not remitted many Years Arrears of Rent, if they had not waited a great while for Money due for Lands, and suffer'd the People to supply themselves with Slaves, before they paid it; if they had not sold their Lands, and established their Rents, at so moderate a Rate; the Country had not been in Circumstances to purchase all the Effects brought yearly from *Great Britain,* in 22 Sail of Ships, as they now do.

[47] The Method has hitherto often been for Men to settle themselves upon a Piece of Ground, improve it, build, raise, stock, plant Orchards, and make such Commodities, which being sold, procur'd them Slaves, Horses, Household-Goods, and the like Conveniences; and after this was done, in seven or eight Years they might begin to think it Time to pay the Lords something for their Land.

Tenure of Lands.

Free and common Soccage is the Tenure by which Lands are held,[25] a small Quit-Rent being paid annually to the Proprietors, as Lords of the Fee, in lieu of all Services, Perquisites, and Demands whatsoever. There are two Ways of taking out Titles; one is by Purchase, at twenty Pounds a thousand Acres, paid to the Lord[']s Receiver, the Grant whereof reserves to their Lordships an annual Rent of a Shilling for each hundred Acres;[26] the other is without any Purchase-money paid down, but by taking out a Patent, upon Condition to pay yearly to the Lords Proprietors a Penny for each Acre.[27] Every one is at Liberty to choose which of these Methods he will, tho' the former, being much preferable, is most common.

The Tenour of the Grants of Lands from the Proprietors, runs to this Purpose: First their Lordships['] Title by [48] a Charter from K[ing] *Charles* II. is recited; then, in Consideration of so much Money there acknowledg'd to be received, they sell, alienate, and make over unto *A. B.* his Heirs, &c. a Plantation, containing so many Acres of Land, situate and lying in such a County, and having such a Form and Marks, as appear by the Plan of it annex'd, he or they paying for the same, the Sum of one Shilling yearly, for each hundred Acres, in lieu of all Dues or Demands whatsoever.

When a Person would take up Land, (as we term it) he first views the Place, and satisfies himself that no other has any Property there, and then goes to the Secretary, and takes out a Warrant for the Quantity he desires. Warrants ready sign'd by the Governour are left with proper Blanks in the Secretarie[']s Office, and directed to the Surveyor, impowering him to measure and lay out such a Number of Acres for such a Person, and to return a Plan and Certificate thereof into the Secretarie[']s Office. Then the Secretary files the Certificates, and writes a Grant (the Form whereof is settled by Act of Assembly) which he annexes to the Plan, and carries it next Council Day, into the Council to be sign'd by the Governour, and such of the Council as are Trustees for the Sale of Lands, and sealed with the publick Seal of the Colony. If the [49] Grant is to be for Lands purchas'd, a Record of the Receipt of the Purchase Money by the Lords Receiver, must be produced, as a Warrant for signing the Patent.

Method and Charges of Settling.

If any one designs to make a Plantation, in this Province, out of the Woods, the first thing to be done is, after having cutt down a few Trees, to split Palissades, or Clapboards, and therewith make small Houses or Huts, to shelter the Slaves. After that, whilst some Servants are clearing the Land, others are to be employed in squaring or sawing Wall-plats, Posts, Rafters, Boards and Shingles, for a small House for the Family, which usually serves for a Kitchin afterwards, when they are in better Circumstances to build a larger. During the Time of this Preparation, the Master Overseer, or white Servants, go every Evening to the next Neighbour's House, where they are lodg'd and entertain'd kindly, without any Charges. And if the Person have any Wife or Children, they are commonly left in some Friend's House, till a suitable dwelling Place and Conveniencies are provided, fit for them to live decently.

Time of Settling.

The properest Time to begin a Settlement is in *September*, or, at farthest, before the first of *December*. The Time between that and the first of *March* is [50] spent in cutting down and burning the Trees, out of the Ground, design'd to be sowed that Year, splitting Rails, and making Fences round the Corn Ground and Pasture. The smallest Computation usually made is, that each labouring Person will, in this Time, clear three Acres fit for Sowing.

In the second Fall, or Winter, after a Plantation is settled, they make Gardens, plant Orchards, build Barns, and other convenient Houses. The third or fourth Winter, Persons of any Substance provide Brick, Lime, or other Materials, in order to build a good House. The Lime here is all made of Oister-shells, burnt with Wood; of these there is great Plenty lying in and by all Creeks and Rivers, in great Heaps or Beds, where large Boats are loaden at low Water.

Our Cows graze in the Forests, and the Calves being separated from them, and kept in Pastures, fenced in, they return home at Night to suckle them. They are first milk'd, then shut up in a Fold all Night, milk'd again in the Morning, and then turn'd out into the Woods. Hogs rove several Miles over the Forests, eating such Nuts and Ground-Roots as they can find; but having a Shelter made at home to keep them warm, and something given them to eat, they generally return every Evening.

[51] People who design to make their Fortunes in new Countries, should consider beforehand, what Method, or Course of Life, they purpose to follow, when they arrive there; and not flatter themselves with vain Fancies, as if Riches were to be got without Industry, or taking suitable Methods to attain them. 'Tis Encouragement sufficient for a rational Man to know, that when due Means are us'd, they seldom fail of obtaining the End. In this Province as little will serve to put a Person into a Way of living comfortably, as in any Place whatever, and perhaps less. That you and your Friends may be th[o]roughly convinc'd of this, without being led into any Mistakes, I shall here first insert an Account of what is necessary to settle a Planter to live with Comfort and Decency; and next, a List of what is sufficient to settle an Estate of 300 *l.* a Year, from which you may proportion other Conditions of Life as you please.

In order to live comfortably, after a Man's own and Family's Passage is paid, and Cloaths bought for the first Year or two, he must have,

[52] *Charges of Settling an Estate of above 30* l. *a Year.*

2 Negro Slaves, 40 *l.* each	80 *l.*
4 Cows and Calves, 1 *l.* 5 *s.* each	5
4 Sows, 15 *s.* each. A Canoe 3 *l.*	6
A Steel Mill, or Pair of Querns,	3

Axes, Hoes, Wedges, Hand-saws, Hammers, and other Tools,	2
200 Acres of Land 4 *l.* Survey and other Charges 2 *l.*	6
A small House for the first Year or two,	8
Corn, Pease, Beef, Pork, *&c.* for the first Year,	14
Expenses and Contingencies,	26
	150 *l.*

This Calculation is made in the Money of the Province, which is just 100 *l.* Sterling.

The Things mention'd here are of Necessity to one who would settle with any tollerable Decency. And from this small Begin[n]ing, by moderate Industry, accompanied with the Blessing of Heaven, a Man may get a competent Estate, and live very handsom[e]ly. But there are many who settle without any Slaves at all, but labour themselves.

Here follows an Account of what is necessary to settle an Estate of 300 *l. per Annum*, with the Value of the Particulars, as they are most commonly sold there.

[53] *Charges of Settling* 300 *l.* per Annum.

30 Negroes, 15 Men and 15 Women, 40 *l.* each	1200 *l.*
20 Cows and Calves, 1 *l.* 5 *s.* each	25
2 Mares, 1 Stone-horse, 10 *l.* each, 6 Sows and a Boar 6 *l.*	36
1000 Acres of Land, 20 *l.* Survey and other necessary Charges 7 *l.*	27
A large Periagoe 20 *l.* a small Canoe 2 *l.* a Steel Mill 4 *l.*	26
10 Ewes and a Ram 7 *l.* 3 dozen Axes 6 *l.*	13
Hoes, Hatchets, Broad Axes, Nails, Saws, Hammers; Wedges, Maul Rings, a Froe, and other necessary Tools.	23
Ploughs, Carts, with their Chains and Irons,	10
A small House for the first Year or two, afterwards a Kitchen.	20

300 Bushels of *Indian* Corn and Pease, at 2 *s.* 6 *d. per* Bushel, with some Beef, Pork, &c. for the first Year[']s Provision,	50
Expences and Contingencies,	70
Total	1500 *l.*

This Sum of *Carolina* Money being reduc'd to Sterling, makes 1000 *l.*

The 30 Negroes beginning to work in *September* or *October*, will clear 90 Acres of Land, plant and hoe it; half of which, that is 45 Acres, sowed with Rice, will, after the common Computation, yield [54] 1000 Weight an Acre, which sold at 15 *s.* a hundred, the middle Price, amounts to 337 *l.* 10 *s.* The other 45 Acres are to be sowed with *Indian* Corn, Pease, Pompions, Potatoes, Melons, and other Eatables, for the Use of the Family.

I am so far from exceeding due Bounds in this Calculation, that I don't by much come up to what I know is annually done by many. This shows the very great Difference between purchasing an Estate of Land in *England*, and settling one in this Province. For the Sum of 1000 *l.* laid out in *England*, at 20 Years Purchase, will buy but 50 *l.* a Year, and here it settle[s] 337 *l.* 10 *s. per Ann[um]* Money of this Colony, which is 225 *l.* Sterling, besides maintaining a House in great Plenty, with most Sorts of Provisions necessary for Life. And to give the larger Allowance, I have not inserted the Profit to be made in remitting the 1000 *l.* in proper goods, but have reckon'd it as brought hither in Specie.

As for those who have no Substance to bring with them, they are either Labourers or Tradesmen, for whose Satisfaction I shall insert the usual Wages and Prices of Labour.

[55] *Price of Labour.*

		s. d.
A Tailor		05:00
A Shooe-maker		02:06
A Smith	hath *per Diem*	07:06
A Weaver		03:00
A Bricklayer		06:00
A Cowper		04:00

A Carpenter and Joiner have from 3 to 5 s.
A Day-Labourer from 1 s. 3 d. to 2 s. with Lodging and Diet.
Those who oversee Plantations *per Ann[um]* from 15 to 40 l.

Proper Season for Coming Hither.

The best Time for *Europeans* to arrive here, in respect to Health, is *September;* for then they have eight Months moderate Weather, before the Heat comes, in which Time the Climate will become agreeable.

If a considerable Number of People should form a Design of coming hither, to settle in a Community or Neighbourhood, it would be proper to send Agents beforehand, to chose convenient Lands, and purchase Corn, and other Necessaries. And if these made a common Plantation, at the Charges of a Joint-Stock, a Year or two before the Arrival of the others, about the Middle of the Place where they design'd a Settlement, and stock'd it with 20 Negroes, Cows, Hogs, &c. it would be very useful to shelter and receive their Friends upon their first Landing; the Sick, likewise, might be there taken Care of, [56] and the poor supplied with Corn for their first Year's Provision; of all which Accounts might be kept, and Payments made, when they that received it grew able.

This Country, perhaps, may not abound so much with those gay and noisy Amusements, which generally the great and rich affect; but for such who have experienc'd the Frowns of Fortune, and have yet something left to make a handsome Retreat from the World; for those who affect Solitude, Contemplation, Gardening, Groves, Woods, and the like innocent Delights of plain simple Nature, and who, with a small Fortune, would provide some competent fix'd Settlement for themselves and Children; there can scarce any Place in the *British* Dominions be found, that will better answer their Expectation. As there are no Beggars among us, so we cannot pretend there are any vastly rich, few Estates exceeding 1000 or 1200 l. a Year, and from thence gradually down to 30 l. Most of us enjoy that State of Life which many People reckon the happiest, a moderate Subsistance, without the Vexation of Dependance.

Advantage of this Province to Great Britain.
When I consider of what Importance this Colony may be in time
to the *British* Nation, the Great Quantities of their Manufactures it
might take off, and the [57] Variety of Commodities which it is
capable of producing, to make suitable Returns; I am perfectly
surprised there should not be the least Care taken to encrease the
Number of its Inhabitants. If the small Number here at present
employs two and twenty Sail of *English* Ships, besides sixty
smaller vessels from other Parts; to what Height may the Trade be
brought, if the People were fifty times the Number they are now,
which the Country would easily contain?

The Scituation of this Province is such as not to interfere with
England, in any Branches of its Manufacture; there is no Mon[e]y
requir'd to be sent hither; it is capable of producing many
Commodities, which are now brought from other Nations, by
Money exported from *England*. The Government may always
regulate the Trade as they please, which they cannot do in foreign
Dominions, but by Treaty and Consent.

South Carolina may be made useful to *Great Britain*, if the
Lords Commissioners of Trade, would please to concert Measures
for sending hither all, or at least some of the most necessary
Commodities which the Country is capable of producing. For
which End, it might not be amiss to consult the Growth and
Product of such Countries, as lie in or near the same Latitude, and
from Correspondents [58] there, as Consuls or Merchants, to get
Seeds of each Kind well preserv'd, and as soon as possible remit
them to *Carolina*; such, for instance, as Almonds, Dates, Olives of
several Kinds, Coffee, Tea, great Variety of Grape-Stones, all
Sorts of Drugs from *Barbary, Persia, Egypt, Syria, &c.* Persons
might likewise be sent over, who are perfectly skill'd in making
Potash, and others expert in framing mechanical Engines, as
Saw-mills to go with the Wind, and the like.

Moreover, 'tis to be wish'd, that upon the Conclusion of this
War, the Government would erect a Fund for transporting
annually hither, for some Years, 100 Families, of the poorer Sort
of People, suppose but of three Persons, one with another, either
of their own Nation or Foreigners, and furnish them with
Necessaries to help them in Settling, and for their Support the
first Year; which would amount to about 20 *l.* Sterling a Head.

That the Kingdom would soon find its Account in this, I shall endeavour to demonstrate, by computing what Advantage 'twould receive in 20 Years, by sending 100 Families, or 300 Persons, whereof we will suppose but 100 are Men. I shall not here proceed in that extravagant Manner, usual with some in Calculations of this Kind, but observe such a Medium as must be grant[59]ed to be very moderate, by all who consider the Matter. Wherefore, to give yet the greater Allowance, I will suppose for the present, that white Women and Children are of no Advantage, (tho' 'tis not altogether so) and only reckon Men fit to Labour, and the Slaves of both Sexes.

I consider, then, no other Advantage the first seven Years, but that each Family hath purchas'd four Slaves; and suppose of themselves to be diminish'd by Death ten in a hundred, so that at the End of seven Years, the Account will stand thus:

White Men	90
Slaves of both Sexes	360
Labouring People	450
The lowest Computation usually made is, that each labouring Person here goes, one	5
with another, add 5 *l.* yearly to the Wealth of *Great Britain,* which, in the whole, is *per Annum,*	2250 *l.*

About the twentieth Year there will be an Addition both to the Whites and Slaves, by Propagation and Purchase, of about fifty in the hundred; wherefore [60] the Account of the yearly Advantage to *Great Britain,* will then stand thus:

White Men	135
Slaves of both Sexes	540
Labouring People	675
	5
These at 5 *l.* each *per Annum,* will, in the whole, yield to *Great Britain* the annual Sum of	3375 *l.*

At the End of the first seven Years, the profit of the Year ensuing has been computed at

	2250 *l.*
In the 20th Year at	3375
Which together make	5625
And half being taken for a Medium of the annual Advantage, is	2812 *l.* 10 *s.*
This multiplied by the Number of Years from 7 to 20, *viz.* 13,	13
Amounts to	36562 *l.* 10 *s.*
Advantage in the whole 20 Years.	

Tho' the Value of what such a Settlement may be afterwards worth cannot well be computed, yet to make some [61] small Estimate, I shall suppose the aforesaid 300 Persons, their Slaves, improv'd Lands and Descendants, to be worth to the *British* Nation, only after the common Value of Estates in Land, at 20 Years Purchase.

	l.	*s.*
Yearly Value the 20th Year	3375 :	00
	20	
Real Value at 20 Years Purchase }	67500 :	00
Advantage of the whole first 20 Years }	36562 :	10
Total	104062 :	10

This certainly is Profit sufficient to encourage them to lay out 6000 Pounds, and that not in Money, but in Freight, Cloaths, Tools, and other Necessaries, which is no great Loss to the Kiingdom[*sic*] in general, only a Charge to the Government.

Having calculated the Benefit accruing to the *British* Nation, for laying out 6000 Pounds, to be at the End of 20 Years 36562 Pounds, 10 Shillings, in Money already received, and a real Estate settled, worth at least 67500 Pounds, I shall now compute what

Advantage the Proprietors will make, which the first seven Years is nothing.

[62] At the End of 7 Years   90 Families
On the 20th Year   135

   Together   225

Half of which being taken
  for a Medium is   112

    I suppose then in the 13th Year, which is the Medium between 7 and 20, every Family buys 400 Acres of Land

> 112 Families
>   400
> 44800 Acres

	l.	*s.*
These 44800 Acres, at 20 *l.* a Thousand, come to	896 :	00
The Yearly Rents at 20 *s.* 1000 Acres, for 7 Years, *viz.* from the 13th to the 20th Year	313 :	12
The Lords have receiv'd at the End of twenty Years	1209 :	12
The Real Value of these 44800 Acres, yielding 44 *l.* 16 *s. per Ann[um]* at 20 Years Purchase comes to	896 :	00
The whole	2105 :	12

[63]

	l.	*s.*
Subtract a fourth Part for Loss, Expences in receiving, and the necessary Charges of the Government, there will then remain	1579 :	04

This compared with the Profit already computed to redound to the Kingdom, is almost the sixty sixth Part thereof, and just that Proportion of Charges, according to the strict Rules of Justice, the Lords Proprietors of *Carolina* should allow for carrying on a Design of transporting People, and rendering the Country more useful and profitable to the *British* Nation than it is at present.

Thus, Sir, I have endeavour'd, in as few Words as I could, to acquaint you with what I think is most requisite for you to know, relating to this Province. I might easily have swell'd my Letter to a regular Treatise, but fearing to be tedious, have left many Things untouch'd, and could not well say less, without falling short in giving you that Satisfaction you desire, and which it will always be my Ambition you should receive from me, in whatever Demands you are pleas'd to lay upon,

  SIR,

Charlestown,
 June 1, 1710   *Your, &c.*

NOTES

1. The early charters are conveniently reprinted in Mattie Erma Parker and William S. Price, Jr., eds., *Colonial Records of North Carolina* (Raleigh, 1963–), 2d ser., I: *Charters and Constitutions of North Carolina, 1578–1698,* 76–104.

2. William, second Lord Craven (1688–1711), was the great-grandson of the cousin of William, First Lord Craven and inherited the first Earl's proprietary share. Henry Somerset, second Duke of Beaufort (1684–1714), acquired the original Monck share in Carolina from his mother whose second husband was John Grenville, Lord Granville, heir to the Monck estate. John Carteret, Earl Granville (1690–1767), was the great-grandson of Sir George Carteret, one of the original proprietors. Sir John Colleton (1669–1754) was the grandson of Sir John Colleton, one of the original proprietors. Maurice Ashley (1675–1726) was a younger brother of the third Earl of Shaftesbury. Although Ashley represented his brother at meetings of the proprietors, he did not himself become a shareholder until the death of the third Earl in 1713. John Danson (d. about 1724) was deeded the original William Berkeley share by his father-in-law John Archdale who in turn had purchased it from Thomas Amy. Joseph Blake Jr. (1700–1751) had inherited the original John Berkeley, Baron Berkeley, share from his father Joseph. The latter had bought the share from Thomas Archdale whose father, John, had bought it in his son's name after the death of the original proprietor in 1678. For more detailed information concerning the proprietors see William S. Powell, *The Proprietors of Carolina* (Raleigh, 1963).

3. The proprietors' powers as defined by the Fundamental Constitutions can

be followed in Parker and Price, eds., *Charters and Constitutions*, 139, 157, 171, 192, 214–15, 234.

4. The election law in force in 1710 is published in Thomas Cooper and David J. McCord, eds., *The Statutes at Large of South Carolina*, 10 vols. (Columbia, 1836–41), II, 79–80.

5. The South Carolina Commons House's control over revenue officers is discussed in Jack P. Greene, *The Quest for Power: The Lower Houses of Assembly in the Southern Royal Colonies, 1689–1776* (Chapel Hill, 1963), 224–33.

6. In fact, formal declaration that English Common Law was in force in South Carolina, except in so far as repealed by statute, came only in 1712. See Cooper and McCord, eds., *Statutes*, II, 413–14.

7. The law referred to is printed in Cooper and McCord, eds., *Statutes*, II, 74, 399–400.

8. This law can be found in Nicholas Trott's Laws, Manuscript volume, South Carolina Archives (Columbia), 54–61. See also Commons House Journals, South Carolina Archives, I, 325–28.

9. The courts of justice act in force in 1710 can be found in Cooper and McCord, eds., *Statutes*, II, 74–76.

10. For a description of the emergence and development of the Court of Chancery in South Carolina see Anne King Gregorie and J. N. Frierson, eds., *Records of the Court of Chancery of South Carolina, 1671–1779* (Washington, D.C., 1950), 3–54.

11. For regulations concerning this court, see Cooper and McCord, eds., *Statutes*, II, 166–67.

12. The relevant statute is in ibid., 120–21.

13. The militia law is published in ibid., IX, 625–31.

14. On this point, see ibid, VII, 33.

15. The War of Spanish Succession, 1701–13.

16. The town of St. Augustine was captured in 1702 by a force led by Governor James Moore. See Charles W. Arnade, *The Seige of St. Augustine in 1702* (Gainesville, 1959), and Verner W. Crane, *The Southern Frontier, 1670–1732* (Durham, N.C., 1929), 75–78.

17. The expedition against the Apalachee Indians in 1704 was also led by Moore. See Crane, *Southern Frontier*, 79–80.

18. South Carolina's early paper money laws are published in Cooper and McCord, eds., *Statutes*, II, 206–12, 229–32, 259, 263–64, 274–77, 302–306.

19. See ibid., 275.

20. See ibid., 200–206, 223, 247–48, 280, 295–97.

21. The act referred to was 6 Queen Anne, c. 30. Passed in 1708, this statute was intended to give Parliamentary authority to a royal proclamation issued in 1704 forbidding the colonies to inflate the value of foreign coins by more than one third. This subject is discussed in Curtis P. Nettels, *The Money Supply of the American Colonies Before 1720* (New York, 1964), 242–49.

22. These laws are printed in Cooper and McCord, eds., *Statutes*, II, 58–60, 131–33, 251–53. It should be noted, however, that by two acts of the Assembly of 1704 aliens were forbidden to sit as members of the assembly. See Cooper and McCord, eds., *Statutes*, II, 251, 253.

23. These regulations may be found in Cooper and McCord, eds., *Statutes*, II, 116–17, 135–36.

24. See ibid., 251–53.

25. This was by the terms of the original Charter. See Parker and Price, eds., *Charters and Constitutions*, 78.

26. This process is illustrated in Records in the British Public Record Office Relating to South Carolina, 36 vols., South Carolina Archives, III, 142.

27. Under the headright system those receiving grants were required to pay a quitrent of a penny an acre. For the most complete description of land policy under the proprietary see R. K. Ackerman, "South Carolina Colonial Land Policies," unpublished PhD. diss., University of South Carolina, 1965.

Pamphlet
Two

PROFITABLE
ADVICE

FOR

RICH and POOR

in a

Dialogue, or Discourse

Between

James Freeman, a *Carolina* Planter

AND

Simon Question, a *West-Country* Farmer.

CONTAINING

A Description, or true Relation

OF

South Carolina

AN

English Plantation, or Colony, in *America:*

WITH

Propositions for the Advantageous Settlement of People, in
General, but especially for the Laborious poor, in that Fruitful,
Pleasant, and Profitable Country, for its Inhabitants

[JOHN NORRIS]

Enter'd in the Hall-Book, according to Law.
London Printed by J. How, in *Grace-Church-street*, 1712; and Sold
in Parcels by *Robert Davis*, Bookseller, in *Bridgewater, Somersetshire*,
and by [*Charles Walkden* at the Bell] in [*New-Fish-Street*,
near *London-Bridge*] with Gilt Forrels   Price 1 *s.* 6 *d.*

[3] To Town and Country Shopkeepers, Parish-Clerks, Innkeepers, or Masters of Publick-Houses.

I t is not altogether, or purely for Self-Interest, and only to promote Sale for these Books, that this is recommended to your several Cares to procure a few of these to be carefully dispos'd of amongst the Customers, or Parishoners, to whom you may, severally, have Opportunity so to do, and altho' it is not your common Business in that Nature, and you are not hereunto inclinable, by reason your own present Profit, by the Sale of a few is of small Value, yet you are desir'd hereunto, in Order that you may (as probably you will) thereby become Instrumental to the future Benefit of some one of your poor Neighbours, in whose Behalf, and for whose Sake, this is chiefly (recommended, requested, or) desir'd from you: And for the better Conveniencies of having [4] these Books dispers'd for the Publick Good amongst those People who might most probably reap the Benefit that is design'd them in Publishing hereof, therefore you are desir'd, frequently, to recommend it to your Neighbours and Friends, as well Rich as Poor, particularly to those that you foresee may reap Profit and Delight in Perusing it, who may be farther Beneficial to the Poor's Advantage, by their Advice and Assistance; Advise them to Buy, that they may have it in their Custody to read at their Pleasure, and that they, thereby, may, at Leisure, consider the Prospect they have in View of making it Advantageous to themselves or others, if they please, by the Knowledge of what is herein contain'd. If, by such your Recommendation and Sale of a few of these Books, any one is pleasur'd and profited, as is the Design hereof, you'll thereby contract a Debt to you for your Care herein (that requires a treble Acknowledgment with Thanks) due from them, the Author and your

Bookseller[1]

The Author, To Church-Wardens, Overseers of the Poor, and Paymasters to their Relief.

Gentlemen,

I Writ and Publish'd this Book for several Reasons: One, and the most material, was my Desire to promote, what in me lies, the future Benefit of many poor, honest, laborious, and industrious People, that here suffers Hardships, with whom it would be much worse, were it not for your several Assistances. I shall recommend this to your deliberate Considerations, in Hopes the real Truths herein contain'd will not otherwise be censur'd; and that many Poor may thereby reap future Advantage, if encourag'd and assisted thereunto in such Methods as appears also for your own Advantage, which is very apparent it will prove to be in Time, if, by your Assistance, such honest Families removes themselves from you, whom otherwise [6] must continue (in Probability them and some of theirs) as a lasting and standing Charge on the Parishes to which they belong; therefore, tho' you may not incline your selves to take a remote Country for your Habitation, by reason the World and Fortune smiles on you at Home, yet you would, I think, shew a good generous Christian Temper to recommend, and further, by your Advice and Assistance, such of your Acquaintance as are requir'd through Misfortunes, (or Want of Ability) and are necessitated to live poor and mean here, and to labour and fare hard at Home for a bare Maintenance of themselves and Families; and perhaps their utmost laborious Care cannot support their Necessities without your publick or private Assistances, which, by this means, may be prevented, and they attain to live Plentiful, and in few Years become of good Substance and Worth, and of sufficient Ability to requite their Friends['] Courtesie in Furthering them thither: By which, you not only ease and prevent Parish Charges; become Instrumental to the present Profit, and future Benefit of [7] such poor People and their Successors, but also to the publick Good, and future Profit of the Crown and Kingdom: And as for many who are here in indifferent good Circumstances, and lives somewhat satisfy'd with what they already have, yet if such Men did forsee a lawful Means farther to advance themselves in Riches, Honour, and good Repute, and live with greater Plenty and Content, a Man might reasonably think they are negligent of their own Interest, if they neglect to take lawful Measures, or Methods for so doing, in order to attain thereto, by chearfully Undertaking a Voyage thither, and experience the pleasant, profitable, and delightsome Way of Living in that Foreign Fruitful Country, which, undoubtedly, People of a middle, mean, or low and poor Station (whilst here) might there attain unto, whether Tradesmen, Jusment Renters,[2] Husbandmen of small Estates, Labourers, Huswifes, Men or Women Servants, Boys, Girls, and Children. If many reap the Benefit I hereby intend them, I have herein my Desire, and shall hereafter, if desir'd by Letter, directed [8] to be left at the Post-House in *Charl[e]s-Town*, (provided the Postage, Pacquet, or Carriage is by them paid) give any Man what farther satisfactory Answers I can return to such Questions, or any other reasonable Requests that shall be propos'd, in Order to satisfy any that intends, or are desirous to remove and settle there, where I am, by God's Permission, an Inhabitant; and whatever honest industrious People are induc'd to transport themselves thither, thro' this Description, I should gladly become acquainted with, and serviceable to them in my Advice, or otherwise, according to my ability, (if acceptable) to prescribe proper Methods and Place for their satisfactory Settlement, according to their Circumstances, in such Ways as is herein propos'd: In the mean Time I remain a hearty Well-wisher to the Advancement of my honest Well-meaning Countrymen, and shall so continue during Life;

John Norris,

PROFITABLE
ADVICE
FOR
RICH and POOR
in a

Dialogue, or Discourse

Between

James Freeman, a *Carolina* Planter

AND

Simon Question, a *West-Country* Farmer.

James Freeman.   Mr. Question, I am come this Morning to pay you a Visit, and spend an Hour or Two in your Conversation, as we have often heretofore done, to divert and pass away some vacant Time in your Company, and Drink my Mornings-Draught in a Glass of your good Liquor.

[10] Simon Question.   *Mr.* Freeman, *my old Friend and Neighbour, you are heartily Welcome; I am glad to see you return'd to your Native Soil. How far'd you in your Travels Abroad, in Foreign Parts of the World, where you have Lived since you left this Neighbourhood? Pray what diverting, yet true, Relation can you oblige your Friend withal, that may, probably, tend to Profit and Delight, either now, or hereafter? I desire you to Entertain me with a true and faithful Description of that Strange Country wherein you have been an Inhabitant some Years past? Mean while I'll Entertain you with the pleasing Diversion of intermixing our Discourse with a Glass of our Native Liquor, made of the juice of Apples and the Barley Corn: Therefore, pray, before you enter thereon, pledge me this Glass or two of Beer.*

J. Freeman.   Thanks, my Friend: I'll freely Pledge, and Discourse you on these Conditions, and Answer you such Questions as you are desirous to be resolved in. In answer to your Question, *How I far'd Abroad, since I left* Eng[11]land? I tell you, truly, I have Lived with Greater Content and Satisfaction than ever I enjoy'd here, before I went hence, through the whole Course of my Life.

S. Question. *What Country is it you Live in? And in what Part of the World? And how came* English *Inhabitants to Settle there?*

J. Freeman. The Country was Named by King *Charles* the Second, and call'd *CAROLINA,* before which time it was never Inhabited by Christian People: There was none but Heathen *Indians,* that had no knowledge of Almighty God. This Country lies on the Main Continent of *America,* between 29 and 36 degrees North Latitude: And being Discovered, or Found, and taken Possession of in the King of *England's* Name, the said King *Charles* did, on request, Grant, by Patent, the said Country unto Eight of His Friends, or Favourites, (viz.) The Earl of *Clarendon,* the Duke of *Albermarl[e],* Lord *Craven,* Lord *Berk[e]lley,* Lord *Ashley,* Sir *William Berk[e]lley,* Sir *George Cart[e]ret,* and Sir *Peter Colletine,*[3] to whom, and their Heirs, [12] or Assigns, for ever, the said Patent makes them true and absolute Lords Proprietors; and therein appointed to be a Province, and call'd *Carolina,* deriv'd from the King's Name.

It is now divided into Two Parts, distinguished by the Names of *North* and *South Carolina. North Carolina* borders on the Southward of *Virginia;* and *South Carolina* borders to Southward on the *Spanish* Ter[r]itories, near that Place call'd *St. Augustine.* It is computed to be, from *North* to *South,* along the Seashore, six or seven hundred Miles, and as much, or more, from the *Eastern* Sea-shore, backward to the *West;* yet but a very Small Part of this Large Country, in proportion to the Whole, is Peopled with Christian Inhabitants, there being not yet Five Thousand Families settled therein. It is now about Forty Years since the Lords Proprietors of the said Province, did first send thither People to Inhabit, since which Time they Yearly encrease by resort of these People thither, who have had a Description of, and was desirous to possess that Fertile Soil. For the Encouragement thereof, these Inhabitants [13] that resort thither may have Land granted them from the *Lords Proprietors* on very easy and cheap Terms; One Hundred Acres there to be bought for less Money than Ten Acres here, and yet Ten Acres there, well Husbanded in proper Grain of that Country, will produce more Profit than Twenty Acres here, in the general Way of Husbandry.

S. Question. *What Country-People have you there, besides* English, *more than the Native* Indians, *and of what Religion?*

J. Freeman. There is, besides *English,* several *Welsh, Scotch, Irish,* and *French Protestants,* and of several Sorts of *Sects* or *Dissenters,* as here, but especially the *Presbyterians,* and *Anabaptists,* and some *Quakers.*

S. Question. *What Religion is most establish'd there; and how are the Ministers of each maintain'd, if you have any?*

J. Freeman. By the King's *Patent,* or *Charter,* People of any Religion might have free *Toleration* to exercise and enjoy the same without Interruption, but the *Church of England* Mi[14]nisters only to be supported and paid by any publick Allowance by Act of *Assembly* or *Parliament* in the said *Province*:[4] In Pursuance whereof, the Parliament of our *Province* of *South Carolina* (to which Part I shall chiefly confine my Discourse) have, of late Years, divided the Inhabited Part of the Country into Parishes, and caus'd Churches to be built, and Parsonage-Houses, and Two or Three Hundred Acres of Gleeb Land thereto, and allow'd to the Minister of each Parish Church One Hundred Pounds *per Annum,* to be paid out of the *Publick Treasury* of the Country at two entire Payments in the Year; to which the Parishoners add their Yearly Voluntary Subscriptions to the *Minister,* which generally amounts to Fifty or Sixty Pounds *per Annum,* more or less, according as the Minister is approv'd of, and belov'd by his Parishoners;[5] for [neither] they nor the *Dissenters* pay no Tythes there: The *Dissenting Ministers* hath only the Voluntary Contributions of their Congregations, so that, I think, I may properly say the *Church of England* is the Superiour; tho' the [15] Churches are not yet all supply'd with *Church of England Ministers*; it has been computed that the *Church of England* People are about Four Tenths of the Number of the Inhabitants; the *Presbyterians* about Two Tenths; *Anabaptists* One Tenth, *French Protestants* Two Tenths; and *Quakers,* and other Religions, One Tenth.

S. Question. *What Method have you there to entitle a* Minister *of the* Church of England *to a Parish to receive these Benefits; and, if once entitled thereto, doth it continue during Life, or only during Pleasure?*

J. Freeman. When a *Minister* comes thither with Permission and License from the Bishop of *London*, after he hath receiv'd the Queen's Bounty of *20. l.* to defray his Expences thither, which ought first to be taken; then, after he is become acquainted with, and approv'd of, by the Parishoners of the Vacant Parish, they voluntarily make Choice of, and Elect, publickly, the said *Minister*, by Subscribing an Instrument in Writing to that Purpose, which being return'd to the Office appointed to receive the same, the said *Minister*, [16] from that Time, is entitl'd to the said Benefice, not to be thereof again depriv'd without Regular Proceedings against him, in Case he misbehaves himself, as in such Cases they are liable to in *England*, and on no other Means or Causes are they to be displac'd.

S. Question. *What Profit may this Parsonage-House and Land be worth to the* Minister *Yearly; and what are your Churches and Houses built withal?*

J. Freeman. The Churches and Parsonage-Houses are generally built with Brick, some with Timber only, and plaister'd within, for there is not Stones to build, as here: As to the Parson's Gleeb Land, the Profit thereof is according to the Stock he keeps, and the Family of Servants, or Slaves, to Work thereon, to raise the Profits from the same by Corn, Rice, or other Grain; for People are not yet populous enough to Rent Land as here, thereby to make Yearly Advantage from the Parsonage and Gleeb Land.

S. Question. *Who are these* Slaves *you speak of? And why are they so* [17] *call'd? What Slavery are they oblig'd unto? And in what Manner are they kept by their Masters?*

J. Freeman. Those we call *Slaves*, are a sort of Black People, here commonly call'd *Blackmoor's*, some few kept here in

England, by Gentry, for their Pleasure, but are there bought by the Inhabitants, from the Merchants Trading to *Guinea*, and other Places, where they are first brought from; but their proper Names are *Negroes*. These People are bought to Employ them in any sort of Labour, either in Town or Country, in what ever their Masters, or Owners, have occasion to be done; the Townsman for his Business, and the Country Farmer, which we call there Planters, about their Husbandry, or Houswifery Business, as Servants are here requir'd to do for their Masters or Mistresses. When these People are thus bought, their Masters, or Owners, have then as good a Right and Title to them, during their Lives, as a Man has here to a Horse or Ox, after he has bought them: And there is a Necessity for these Slaves, because [18] very few Servants are there to be procured to perform the Business of the Country. There is also another sort of People we buy for Slaves, call'd *Indians*, bred on the Continent, but far distant from us, belonging to the *French* and *Spanish* Tearitories in *America;* they are a sort of Red Dun, or Tan'd Skin'd People, who are also Sold us by Merchants, or Traders, that deal with several Nations of our Native *Indians*, from whom they first buy these People, whom we then make Slaves of, as of the *Negroes;* and they are call'd Slaves, not because their Labour is more Slavish or Servile than Servants['] Labour is here, nor often times so hard to perform as the Labour requir'd from Servants in this Country, but 'tis, because they are never Free-Men, or Women, during their Life, nor their Children after them, who are under the same Circumstances of Servitude as their Parents are, during their Lives also.[6]

S. Question.   *But do not* English *People, and others, when they come first into the Country, become Slaves* [19] *There, as it is generally said they do in other* English *Plantations in* America?

J. Freeman.   No; there is, of a Truth, no such Thing as *Christian Slaves*, made of People coming from any part of the Queen's Dominions; for that which is generally talk'd, of People[']s being made Slaves, is no more but this, When any Men or Women, that are desirous to Transport themselves thither, and are not of Ability to pay their own Passage over, they are generally oblig'd, by Indentures, before their Departure hence, to serve in that Country, as Servants or Apprentices do here, for the Term of Four Years, to commence from the Time of their Arrival, and no longer; their Masters or Mistresses, in the mean Time, giving them sufficient Cloathing, and other Necessaries, or Paying them sufficient Wages so to do; and at the Four Years End they are then become free from their Service, and no Man can longer detain them, they being then at Liberty to follow what lawful Business they please to undertake to their own Advantage and Satisfaction.

[20] S. Question. *But I suppose the Labour, both of Men and Women Servants, is, generally, more servile and laborious than here in England, whether for Husbandry or Huswifery Business as the Country affords?*

J. Freeman. Their Labour there is not, in Reality, as hard as it is generally in *England* for Men nor Women; neither, as I mention'd before, do our Slaves undergo the Hardships that many Thousand Servants, and poor Laboure[r]s, do in *England, Wales, Scotland,* and *Ireland,* which those that comes from these Places as Servants doth find by common Experience.

S. Question. *I would desire you to relate to me the Kinds of Labour there for Men and Women; But first, if you please, acquaint me with the Nature of the Climate, the Soil, and Productions of the Country; what Sorts of Timber you have; and what Sorts of Grain is most usual amongst you: But, before you enter thereon, let us take a hearty Glass of Syder, for Discourse is dry: Come, Friend, here's to you a full Bumper.*

[21] J. Freeman. I'll heartily pledge you, and then proceed. The Country lies, as I told you before, between 29 and 36 Degrees *North* Latitude, and, as I guess, *South West* from the Land's End of *England,* and about Eleven Hundred Leagues distant from thence, which causes the Climate to be hotter there than here in *England,* especially in the Months of *June, July,* and *August,* but the rest of the Year is very moderate, not too hot, nor never such violent Frosts as here; seldom or never that Snow falls and lies there to cover the Ground: We have in *December* and *January* some small Frosts, generally, in the Night, and Thawing next Day when the Sun rises; it is a great Rarity to find a Frost continue two or three Days at a Time, but in these Months we have some cold and sharp *North West* Winds, which comes from the frozen Lake of *Canady*, of which we are very apprehensive, but at the Change of the Winds we soon find it warm and pleasant Weather: *February* and *March* are, generally, fair, pleasant, [22] and dry Months, only some Showers answering in Temperature to *April* and *May* in *England*, and them Months, like *June* and *July*, but refresh'd often with Showers, and then presently fair and clear Weather: *September, October*, and *November* are pleasant Dry Months. The greatest Part of the Year round seems very pleasant and delightful, and is generally Healthful to most People that live Temperate, and not drink Immoderately, or use immoderate Exercises, thereby destroying Health, and too often their Life also. Although the Summer Months seem burthensome to some People, yet the Conveniency of shady Groves, open Air, Arbours, Summer-Houses, and frequent cool Bathings makes amends sufficiently for the Inconveniency. The Country where it is yet Inhabited along the Sea-shore, and near 200 Miles back, is plain and level Land, few Rising Hills above 30 Foot higher than the lowest Land; the Soil is generally Sandy, but of differing Colours, under which, Two or Three Foot Deep, is Clay of which good [23] Bricks are made. It naturally produces many Sorts of Timber and Shrubs, usual in *England*, and many more not Growing here. There are several Sorts of Oak, distinguish'd by these several Names, as *White* of Two Sorts, *Red, Spanish, Water*, and *Live Oak*, the latter so call'd, because the Leaves continue green thereon all the Winter, and is esteem'd to be as lasting as the best *English Oak*, but the other Sorts are not: There is *Elm, Ash, Poplar, Mulberry, Wallnut, Beach, Asp*, large *Bay-Trees*, and *Olive, Hickory, Chinkapine, Tulip-Tree, Pomato, Fir, Pine, Cedar, Cyprus, Myrtle, Sasifrax*, and Variety of other Sorts, which I cannot now name.

The Sorts of Grain most useful is several Kinds of *Indian* Corn, which People here call *Virginia Wheat*: There is near Twenty Sorts of *Indian Pease* and *Beans*, some of them very good for Food, exceeding the best *English Pease*. There grows plentifully the best

Rice that is brought to *England* from any Part of the World. We have Two or Three Sorts thereof. *English Wheat, Barley,* [24] *Pease, Oats,* and *Rye* will thrive well there, but the Inhabitants are not yet accustom'd to sow much thereof, for Reasons I shall after acquaint you. We have *Tobacco* which is much esteem'd, and preferr'd before *Virginia Tobacco,* yet not planted for Transportation.

S. Question. *What Sorts of Quick Goods doth the Country produce?*

J. Freeman. Cattle and Swine in Abundance, and Horses Plenty, but as yet Sheep are not plentiful, by reason we have not yet much Land clear'd from Timber and Shrubs, under which Sheep will not thrive well, as Cattle, Horses, and Swine doth there to Admiration.

S. Question. *Then, probably, Beef, Pork, Butter, and Cheese is plentiful?*

J. Freeman. There is Beef and Pork very plentiful, many Thousand Barrels thereof sent off Yearly to the *West-India* Islands, where it is scarce, but, nevertheless, Butter and cheese is not yet plentiful, by reason we have not Plenty of good Huswifes to manage a Dairy, and make it to Advantage, for there is many Thousand [25] Cows in the Country that have never been milk'd for want of People to manage it Advantageously, so that it sells there dearer than in *England,* especially good Cheese at Six, Seven, or Eight-Pence a Pound, sometimes more.

S. Question. *Is your Beef and Pork generally fat there as here, and to be had plentiful at all Times of the Year?*

J. Freeman. Our Beef is Grass fed, and in the latter End of *August* and *September* is very fat, at which Time we kill, barrel, and sell to the Merchants for Transportation; but for Stall fed Beef is not usual, for there is scarce any Hay made in the Country. The Pork is, generally, well fed in the Winter by Acrons [sic], Nuts,

Wild Potatoes, and other Things with which the Woods is well stor'd; but if it proves that they are not so fat as the Owner expects them, they are then sty'd up, and fed on Corn and Pease, and is esteem'd to be as good as *English,* and may be frequently fed for Slaughter at any Time of the Year, but the greatest [26] Quantities are kill'd about *December,* after which Time we kill very little Beef, for then it is fallen in Flesh.

S. Question.   *Have you Poultry there bred on the Farms, or Tenements, as is usually here, by good Huswifes for the Families['] Use? And do your Inhabitants there live as plentifully in Provisions as our Country Farmers and Tradesmen do here?*

J. Freeman.   There is bred on our Plantations (for so we call our Farms) great Plenty of the Several Kinds of Fowl as here, and there kept in great Numbers for their Use; and altho' we have not the Conveniency of Fresh Beef throughout the whole Year, yet we take particular Care to store our Houses with Salt-Beef and Pork 'till Fresh comes again in Kind, with which, and other Sorts of Fresh Provisions, of which we have Plenty; such as Venison, Pig, Pork, Fowl, and Fish, which we have plentiful for such as delight to take them in our Rivers, with which our industrious Planters providing for their Families, enables them to live as plentiful as any temperate Men can desire or expect. It is ge[27]nerally suppos'd that scarce half of our Corn and Pease is expended in the Country, nor one Sixth, or Eighth Part of the Rice, Beef, and Pork spent there, by the Inhabitants, that the Country doth produce.

S. Question.   *If Wheat and Barley is not plentiful, how are you supply'd with Bread, and Beer, for your necessary Occasions in your Families?*

J. Freeman.   The Country Planters that hath not *English* Grain makes Bread for their Families with *Indian* Corn and Rice, of which is made very good Bread, not much Inferiour to your fine Wheaten Bread, especially Rice Bread, whilst new, eats as pleasant, and is as White to compare with the Finest Wheaten

Bread. As for our Drinking, there is little Malt Beer, as yet, brew'd amongst the Country People; there is a pleasant fresh Drink made, to quench Thirst, of Molosses, Barbacude Peaches, and a Fruit call'd *Locust,* and of other Things: Our strong Liquor to drink for Pleasure is *Made[i]ra* Wine, and *Rum,* drank either alone, or compounded, and made into *Sangeree,* or [28] *Punch,* of which many Men delight to drink so much to Excess that destroys their Health, which might otherwise be preserv'd, if they drank moderately, when Occasion requir'd for Refreshment sake.

S. Question. *Have you not some Distempers there peculiar to the Country which is not usual here in* England?

J. Freeman. There is, in the Spring of the Year, a Feaver and Ague seizes many that are settled on the lowest Marsh Land, especially when they are new Comers into the Country, which is commonly call'd a Seasoning to them; after which, if their Habitations is on dry healthy Land, they are, generally, very healthful, if temperate: But there is a Distemper attends many Men, tho' but few Women, which they generally call the *Dry-Belly-ake,* many People say it proceeds from Drinking too much *Rum* and *Punch,* but, whatever is the Cause, it is a violent Pain in the Bowels, which deprives some Men of the Strength and Use of their Hands and Feet, as the Gout often doth here, but it is seldom these [29] Distempers prove mortal, nor of long Continuance, if Timely Care is taken for the Cure: And there is Distempers usual here, which is seldom there, as *Ptisick, Stone, Gout,* and several others.

S. Question. *What Sort of Air have you? Do not these hot Months of* June, July, *and* August *naturally create Feavers and other Distempers to* English *Constitutions, especially to the Labouring People in the violent Heat?*

J. Freeman. Our Air is generally very clear and fine, seldom a Day in a Month, throughout the Year, that we have not the benefit of Sun-shine at some part of the Day, even in the Midst of Winter: It has been Observ'd, that but Eight Cloudy

Overcast Days happen'd in the compass of a Year, in which the Sun did not appear. Our Rains generally falling in hasty, sudden, and hard Showers, not long lasting; and then, forthwith, the Sun dissipates, or disperses the Fogs, and Restores the Air fine and clear. In the Summer we have often hard refreshing Showers, very agreeable, accompanied with [30] Thunder, which is very acceptable, since we find it beneficial, in clearing and purifying the Air. The Labouring People, generally, in the Hottest Weather, for Three or Four Hours in the Middle of the Day, leave their Labour, and Refresh and Divert themselves in Bathing in Cool-Water; and retiring to the Shady Groves, Arbours, or Houses, whereby they allay the violence of the Heat, and keep their Blood and Bodies Cool; and are generally, with care, as free, or clearer from Feavours, and other Sickness, than People are often here in *England:* (except, as aforesaid, at their first Seasoning) And as for those who do not Labour in the Field, they may constantly confine themselves in the Shades, and not expose themselves to the heat of the Sun; but after some time, that People have been accustomed thereto, they do not find the Heat so burthensome, but can well dispence therewith.

S. Question. *But, I suppose, Servants, and Slaves, are not permitted, by their Masters, to spend Time, Daily, thus in Refreshing themselves; they [31] are probably, obliged to follow their Labour, both in Wet and Heat; and I guess, a Servant, if he contradicts his Master[']s pleasure therein, must expect Correction, or Punishment, for any Neglect, or Misdemeanor?*

J. Freeman. It is no Master's Interest to oblige Servants, nor Slaves to Toil and Labour so as to destroy their Health, which will, thereby, prevent the performing of their Daily Labour. If a Man, in the Summer, begins his Labour early in the Morning, as is usual, for the benefit of cool Working, and end late in the Evening, he may well spare time, in the middle of the Day, to Refresh himself. And as for Servants receiving from their Masters undeserved Correction, the Laws of the Country doth protect them, as here; and if, on sufficient Complaint, and Proof, to the Governor, or Magistrates, that they are Abused, they shall be by them set free of the remainder of their Time they have to Serve:

But, nevertheless, Servants are not Tolerated, nor Allow'd, by Law, or Custom, to commit willful and voluntary Offences against [32] their Masters, either in Word or Deed, to their Prejudice.[7]

S. Question. *What? Have you a Governor, and Parliament to make Laws, and Magistrates, and other Officers to see and put the Laws in execution, as is customary in* England?

J. Freeman. We have a Governor, deputed by Commission from the Lords Proprietors of the Province, which, in some Cases, has a resemblance to a King or Queen, in respect of Government; He Commissions Justices of the Peace for each County, and other Officers, Civil, and Military.

At his pleasure, by the approbation of the Council, He Calls or Dissolves the Parliament, or Assembly, which is there chosen by the Freemen of the Province, *(viz.)* all Men that are not under Obligation of Service for a Term, as aforesaid; which Assembly, or Parliament, consisting of Two Houses, doth Enact and Make Laws, by the Governor's Approbation, such as may be most Serviceable for the Public Good, or any By-Laws, for particular Cases, provided they are not contrary, or repugnant to the Laws [33] of *England;* and are, generally, made to Resemble, as near as may well suit with the Place, to the Laws in force here; which Laws are there requir'd to be Observed, and the Offenders therein, when Prosecuted, liable to the like Punishments as here, our Laws being much the same in effect.

S. Question. *Do your Parliament lay Taxes, and Impositions on the Subjects, to help support and maintain the Wars, and other necessary expences of the Crown of* England; *or only for the necessary Uses and Expences of your own Province? Or what proportion may it bear with our Taxes here in* England? *Or do not you esteem our Enemies as yours?*

J. Freeman. Our Parliament, at their pleasure, seeing good cause, may Tax the Country if occasion requires; but we do not pay towards maintaining the publick nor private Occasions of the

Crown of *England*. Our Taxes, if any [there] are, ought to be employ'd only to the Countrie[']s Use. I have not known, or heard of only one Tax, generally throughout the whole Country, which was employ'd to the Fortifying of *Charles* Town, the Chiefest Town in the Province:[8] For the nes[34]secary[*sic*], Occasions of the Publick is supply'd by an Imposition, or Duty, charg'd on Goods Imported or Exported, which is paid into the publick Treasury.[9] And as we are still Subjects to the Crown of *England*, so we esteem the Enemies to *England* as ours, and on all Oppertunities we endeavour to shew our diligence to Offend them, and defend and guard ourselves against their Incursions if they, at any Time, should attempt it: Our Proportion of Taxes, or Impositions, to compare with what they are in *England*, is very small, seeing, as I told you, only Goods exported, and imported, is liable to such Payments, and here I find few Things, necessary for common Use, is exempted from being Tax'd, which is very burthensome to the Subjects.

S. Question. *What Sorts of Goods is generally imported into your Country, from* England, Scotland, *or* Ireland?

J. Freeman. Linnen and Woollen of most Sorts for Cloathing, especially that which is fine; most Sorts of Hous[e]hold Goods; Edge Tools for Tradesmen's Uses; Nails; Axes; [35] Saws; Hoes; and other Tools for Planters['] Use: Guns; Powder; Shot; Bullets; and many Sorts of Necessaries for the *Indians['*] Uses, which I cannot now name.

S. Question. *And what Sorts of Goods do you export, or send off, from thence to* England, *and other Places you Trade withal?*

J. Freeman. Our chiefest Commodities sent here to *England* is our most excellent Rice, of which comes great Quantities; and great Numbers of Deers-Skins sold to our Merchants, or Traders, by the Native *Indians*; also great Quantities of Pitch and Tar; some Rozen, and Turpentine, and Hatters['] Furrs: To the *West-India* Islands, and other Places, is sent Beef; Pork; Tallow; Hides; Leather, Candles; Myrtle and

Bees-Wax; Corn; Pease; Barrel; Hogshead, and Pipe-Staves; Cyprus; Shingles; Cedar; and many other Commodities I cannot, at present, remember.

S. Question. *Pray what is Pitch, Tar, Turpentine, and Rozen made from?*

[36] *J. Freeman.* It all proceeds from the Substance of the Fir, or Pine-Trees; the Tar from the Heart of the dead Pine-Tree, extracted by Burning the Wood like Charcoals here, and afterwards boil'd in a Furnace which makes it into Pitch; The Turpentine proceeds from the living Pine, when wounded or cut in the Sides, from whence it bleeds, or runs out of the Bark, and afterwards by Boyling, becomes Rozen.

S. Question. *Do you Sow, Reap, and Husbandry your Corn, Pease, and Rice, as we do our English Grain?*

J. Freeman. No; it is far differing in all Respects from Seed-Time 'till Harvest.

S. Question. *Pray give me a Description what Way you take to Husbandry your Crops of Grain, and how you manage your Husbandry from the Beginning to the End of the Year; but let us first take a Glass to revive your Spirits, and strengthen, or refresh, your Memory?*

J. Freeman. I'll pledge you freely, and then proceed. You are then to be inform'd, that sup[37]pose a Man is to enter on a new Plot of Wood-Land (as our Land is in general) for his next Year's Crop, he begins to prepare for it in the Beginning of Winter, or about *Michaelmas*, if his other Business permits him; then, with his labouring Family of Slaves and Servants in a proper Plot of Land for the Grain he intends for the same, with Axes, falls, or cuts down the Trees growing thereon about Three Foot high from the Ground, which causes the Roots to die without Springing again, and is also the easier for Men to stand strong at their Work; which done, they with Saws, Mauls, or Bittles, and Wedges, cut and split the Bodies of the Trees into Rails of Eleven or Twelve Foot long, with which the Land is fenc'd or inclos'd; then the Limbs and Boughs of the Trees, together with the small Under-Shrubs, being grub[b]ed, or rooted up, is all cast into Heaps, and, in *February* or *March,* Fire is set to it, and burns it clean up to clear the Land; after which, in any of the Months of *March, April,* or *May,* or a Week in *June, Indian* [38] Corn and Pease may be planted; thus, with a broad Hoe, or Mattock, make a Hole in the Ground about a Foot square, and about Four Inches deep; and in a direct Line at Six Foot Distance another such Hole, and so, in straight Row, throughout the Field in Length; then about Six or Seven Foot Distance on the Side; another such Row, and in like Manner throughout the Field intended to be planted: (for so we call it by reason it is done in such Manner, and not like Sowing of Grain in *England)* the Rows, thus done, stands like the Rows of Trees in an Orchard; then, with the Quantity of little more than an *English* Peck of *Indian* Corn, we plant an *English* Acre of Land by Dropping about Five Grains in each Hole so made, which is cover'd with Part of the Earth dug from thence; then, when the Corn is so planted, we, with our Hoes, which is about nine Inches broad in the Mouth, cut up the Grass, Weed, and Trash, whatever it be that grows in the Field amongst the Corn, the Ground then lying bare, only what is cover'd with [39] the Weeds and Rubbish so cut between the Rows of Corn; then, about a Month after the Corn is planted, we make smaller Holes, with our Hoes, between each Hole of planted Corn, into which we drop Eight or Ten *Indian* Pease, less than an *English* Peck suffices to seed an Acre of Land, which being cover'd very lightly with Earth, the Pease and Corn grows together 'till separated at Harvest, in the mean Time we Hoe or Weed it again, once or twice more, as at first; from which Half Bushel of Corn and Pease as seed to an Acre, we gather in of Pease at Harvest (from an Acre) Twelve or Fifteen Bushels, or more, and Twenty or Twenty Five Bushels of Corn, sometimes more; there has been Forty Bushels of Corn from an Acre, besides Twenty of Pease, which is much greater Increase than here in *England:* We account a good Labouring Man, whether Servant, or Slave, can, in the Compass of a Year, clear, fence, plant, hoe, harvest, and beat out, or thrash, at least, four Acres of Corn and Pease, besides Land planted with Necessaries for the Fa[40]mily's Use, or Three Acres of Rice, also other Things for the Family: As to the Manner of Planting our Rice, after the Land is clear'd or clenged, as aforesaid, we, with Hoes, trench the Land something like Furrows made with a Plough, but not so deep, and about a Foot Distance between each Trench; and when the Land is so Trench'd, in the Month of *April* we seed it, carefully, within each Trench, and cover it thin with Earth, one Peck and Half is sufficient for to seed an Acre, then, with narrow Hoes made for that Purpose, about Five or Six Inches broad in the Mouth, we Hoe, Weed, or cut up the Grass, or other Trash, growing between the said Trenches of Rice, which ought carefully to be done Three Times in the Summer, for Grass and Weeds growing between the Corn, Pease, or Rice, will otherwise destroy or spoil the Crop; Then, at Harvest, which comes in *September,* we reap and carry it to Barns, which, when thrash'd, if it prov'd a good Crop, 30, 35, or 40 Bushels, sometimes more, comes from off one Acre of Land which was [41] seeded with less than Half a Bushel, which is also much greater Increase than any Grain here in *England* doth generally afford; we usually account an Acre of indifferent Rice when mell'd in a Mill, and cleng'd as Oats are here, will yield half a Tun of Rice fit for the Merchants, commonly worth Eighteen or Twenty Shillings the Hundred Weight, besides the small broken Rice for the Family's Use, which is as serviceable as the other, tho' not so vendable.

S. Question. *I find, by your Description, you have extraordinary increase in your Grain; but I do not understand why you work your Land thus with Hoes; would not a Plow be more speedier, and less troublesome? And I observe you mention nothing of Manuring, or Improving your Land for Corn or Rice, nor how many Years you keep it in Hand before you lay it out to Rest, or how long after, before you take it in again to Tillage.*

J. Freeman. We cannot possibly put the Plow in such Land, when so Clear'd as we call it, for the great Bodies that was not us'd in Fencing, [42] the Stumps, and spreading Roots of the Trees, prevents the Plowing it, till it has lain Clear'd for Twelve or Fifteen Years, by which time they'll rot, consume, and moulder to Dust, being expos'd to all Weathers; but we account Three or Four

Years sufficient to Plant (as we call it) one piece of Land, before we lay it out for Grass, and then Clear more, and seldom desire to Plant the same again, but let it lie for Pasture for Sheep and Calves. As for Manuring our Land, we need it not, it is naturally Fertile enough and good to bear our Crops, without Dung, or other Manure. We seldom Manure any Land, except for Garden-Ware, or Pompeons for our Hogs or Swine.

S. Question. *What sort of Kitching-Garden-Ware have you there generally, in the Country Plantations?*

J. Freeman. We have many sorts of small Pot-Herbs, as here, and such as Onions, Leeks, Carrets, Turnips, Parsnips, Potatoes of several kinds, not usual here; we have an excellent Root call'd Eddows; we have Colworts, Savoys, and the like, and se[43]veral other sorts of Greens; some White-Cabbag[e], but not common: We generally Plant great quantities of Pompions, and *West-India* Potatoes, chiefly for our Hogs or Swine, tho' either is very Serviceable and Palletable for a Family of Slaves: I have gather'd Cart-Loads of Pompeons into House for Swine. And have had 150 Bushels of Potatoes from off an Acre of Land, on which I Planted about Five Bushels; I have been told some have had double that Quantity. There is also a very good Boyling Root call'd Yams. We have plenty of several sorts of *Indian* and Kidney-Beans, very pleasant to Eat Green; Squashes, Cowcumbers, and the like. In our fields we Plant large quantities of Musmellons and Water-Mellons, which are much pleasanter to Eat than here: They are a fine cooling pleasant sort of Fruit in the hottest Months; and the overplus, or offel, we throw to our Hogs, and Plant the more of them for that use.

S. Question. *Do you Plant any Fruit-Orchards, or Viniards? And of what Kinds, and Uses?*

[44] *J. Freeman.* Some Men have Planted Viniards, and Orchards of Plumb, Apple, and Pear-Trees, which thrive and bears well, but they are not yet common, tho' they increase by degrees; but it is common to most Planters, to plant in Orchards

quantities of several kinds of Peaches, Nectrons, Maligotoons, Quinces, Apricocks, Figs, and Mulber[r]ys, all which are great bearers, and pleasant to Eat; even the Quinces Eats there as mellow and pleasant as Apples; I have drank a good pleasant Liquor, or Syder made of them; tho', indeed, these Fruits are more frequently Distil'd, from which comes a very strong Spirit, not much inferiour to Rum, or Brandy, in my Judgement. We dry but few of our Figs; they are Eaten when Ripe, in *July*, and *August*, from off the Trees; and some Distil[l] them, others make from them an excellent strong Drink, and pleasant withal, which exceeds, in goodness, most sorts of Wine. From the Viniards has been made good Wine. Our Apple-Orchards bears good Fruit, according to the kind, but we want of [45] the choicest kind to make good Cyder, and for such Fruit as will preserve long in Houses. The Mulberry Trees bears and ripens their pleasant Fruit in May, and the Leaves whereof, in March and April, feed the Silk-Worms, which spins Silk, that is esteemed very fine and strong, of which might be made quantities for Transportation, had we People to Manage it. We having great variety of sorts of Peaches, Nectrons, and Malicotoons, our Orchards affords us some ripe Fruit from the latter end of *June* till the end of *September*. They are Planted in the Stone, and in Three Years will Bear; in Five or Six, become a flourishing and great bearing Orchard. Many Men Plant large Orchards, of many Hundred Trees, chiefly to give the Fruit Daily to their Swine, whilst they are in kind; and the Fruit also being Barbacude, or Dry'd, are servicable for many uses in the Family.

S. Question. *You talk of several sorts of Food you provide for your Hogs, or Swine, by which I suppose you keep many about your Plantations?*

J. Freeman. We find them very [46] Profitable and therefore use all Means we can to raise great Stocks of them, for many Men hath by their Stocks of Cattle and Hogs, in few Years, become Rich; whereas, at their first coming into the Country, or when they became Freemen, could scarce Purchase, at ready pay, a couple of Cows, and Farrowing Sows, to begin a Stock withal.

S. Question. *Why do you talk of a couple of Farrowing Sows for a poor Man to begin withal? That is sufficient for a great Farmer to breed a Stock from.*

J. Freeman. But our Planters find, by Experience, far otherwise, some Men has at their Plantations, 40, 60, 80, or 100 Hogs, or Swine, of all sizes: Nay, some has Two or Three Hundred comes every Evening home to their Sties, at the lowd sound of a Horn, to receive, from their Server, either Corn, Pease, Pompeons, Potatoes, Peaches, or whatever else is allow'd to cause them to remember their Home; but that which is daily given them by Hand, is not sufficient to maintain a Tenth Part of them, were [47] they close confin'd, for they gather their Food in the Woods, of what they find, such as Nuts, Acrons[sic], Roots, wild Fruit, and the like, with which they are frequently Fat, and kill'd about *Christmass,* as I told you before, and Barrel'd for sale, that is, such as are a Year Old, or upwards, at which Age two of them often fill a Barrel and [a] half, worth about three Pounds *per* Barrel, therefore one Man keeps many Farrowing Sows.

S. Question. *Do you keep stocks of Cattle proportionable to your Swine?*

J. Freeman. Men's Stocks of Cattle are proportionable to the Time, since their beginning, and to the quantity and goodness of the Land they feed on. Some Men content themselves with fewer than others; some may not exceed above Thirty, Forty, or Fifty; some Men have One, Two, Three, Four, or Five Hundred *Cattle* at a Time; Others, again, having large Tracts of Land to feed them on, Summer and Winter, keeps a Thousand, or more. I knew a Man, that at his first coming into the Country, was a Servant for Four Years, yet before his [48] Death, it was computed he had at least Three Thousand Head of Cattle, Young and Old; and a Hundred Horses; and Three Hundred Calves Yearly, which he bred, without the trouble and expence of providing Winter Fodder for them; yet, wanting good Huswifes to make Butter and Cheese, had not sufficient, without Buying, for his Family's use, which was not great, Slaves not being allowed that sort of Diet,

101

because of the Scarcity thereof, as yet; But I hope in Time, more good Huswives will be perswaded to come thither to Live, and thereby we shall have plenty of good Butter and Cheese, not only for our own use in the Country, but also to Transport to the *West-India* Islands, where it sells dearer than it is now with us where the common Price of Butter, in the Cask, is Six Pence a Pound, Cheese, as much, or more, especially *English*, at Eight Pence or Ten Pence a Pound, as I told you before.

S. Question. *Then certainly these Men that keep such large Stocks, must,* [49] *of necessity, have very large Quantities of Land to Feed them on.*

J. Freeman. They have so; for the Lords Proprietors of the Province Sells Land very cheap, reserving a small Yearly Rent, by which Means Men attain to great quantities of Land as well as Stock, whereby they are also enabled to purchase many Slaves, which brings them great Profit and Advantage Yearly in Employing them in Planting of Corn, Rice, and the like, as aforesaid, or making Tar, and Pitch, Turpentine, and Rosin, and in Time, thereby become able to build fine Brick Houses.

S. Question. *How say you? The Stock is not provided for with Fodder against-Winter. How then, and what do these great Heards Feed on in that Time?*

J. Freeman. Although we have, almost, incredible Numbers, yet we provide no Fodder for them against Winter, for they gather their Food in the Woods at that Time also, partly on plenty of the Summer Ruffet[Russet]-Grass, and long sort of green Moss, which the Winds shakes off the Trees, where[50]on hungry Cattle will Feed; and I think it may be comparable to very good Straw: But there is a sort of short Cane growing plentifully on the lower moist Land, which bears a long green Leaf in Winter, on which Cattle delight much to Feed; and where that is plentiful, Cattle keeps themselves in very good plight, till Grass springs again.

S. Question. *I admire, that seeing Cattle are so Plentiful, Butter and Cheese should be so Scarce, and Dear, unless your hot Summer Weather is so disagreeable, to hinder those that could, and would, otherwise, make and preserve it good and well.*

J. Freeman. As I told you before, we have but few good industrious Huswifes, as yet, that know well how to Manage it: They are, generally, Women bred up in Cities, Towns, or some other Places where they were not experienced with Dairies, so that they, having not been accustomed thereto, know not how to take the best Methods to make and preserve it good: Yet I have Eaten as good Butter and Cheese, from a good Hus[51]wife[']s Hands, tho' made in the Hottest Seasons, that I think it may be compareable to what is generally made in *England;* and Methods may be taken to preserve it as long without spoiling, in cool, underground Rooms, if we had many careful, knowing, and experienced Women to Manage it for their Profit, Credit, and Advantage.

S. Question. *But suppose good Huswifes came, and did endeavour therein, what Measures should be taken to get the Cows Daily, and Seasonably, at home to Milk, seeing they, generally, Feed abroad in the Woods, and not Fenc'd in Fields, whereby you cannot readily know where, nor when to find them, in order to have them carefully and seasonable Milk'd?*

J. Freeman. We take this Method. In the Spring of the year, when the Cows have Calved, we ride out in search for them in the Woods, and bring them home, then seperating the Cows from the Calves, keeping the Calves Inclos'd, within a good rail-fenc'd Field, of good Grass, for them to Pasture in: Then turning the Cows out, into the Woods a[52]gain, at their liberty, they will return seasonably, in the Evenings, to suckle their Calves, at which time the Milkers may take what quantity of Milk they please from the Cows, only allowing the Calves, during the Summer, as much Milk as may be sufficient to keep the Cows and Calves in love, and to remember each other: And tho' it may be alledg'd, That the Calves thereby deprive the good Huswife of part of her profit, yet, considering the Number of her Cows, which she may very easily encrease at her pleasure, by reason they are bought cheap, and kept cheaper, therefore she may well dispence with that Inconveniency, which proves a Conveniency for the improving of the Breed, by means of Suckling them, till better able to live alone, without Sucking their Dams.

S. Question. *What are the Reasons that your Planters do not Sow more* English *Wheat, Barl[e]y, Pease, and Oats? Since, as you say, it will Thrive well there, that you may have plenty of good Wheaten Bread for a Toast, and Strong Malt-Beer, whereof to Boast; White [53] Pease to your Pork, to make you Strong; and from your Oates, Grets, or great Oatemeal, to help make you good fat Black-Puddings, seeing you kill so many fat Hogs, that you may not appear to live Niggardly, Sloathful, or Hogish your selves?*

J. Freeman. Your jocular question requires the like Answer.

> We esteem not *Puddings* good, in the Guts of Hogs,
> We with such Offal feed *Plantation Dogs;*
> And *Pease,* we know, are good to feed fat Swine;
> Strong Beer, and Toast, to make Men drunk betime;
> If that's the Reasons, we *English* Grain should crave,
> We'll leave it off, and follow those we have:
> For good *Rice-Puddings,* doth it far exceed;
> So does our best white *Callivant Pease* indeed:
> Our *Barbadoes* Rum, and *Made[i]ra* Wine,
> Pleases *Planters* better than Strong Beer that's fine,
> In which we put white *Rice*-Bread Toast,
> If Farmers had such, they'd thereof boast.

But to Answer you seriously, why *English* Grain is neglected, is because it is not so Profitable to the Planter as Rice; for one Acre of good Rice, is as Valuable as two or three Acres of *English* Grain: Neither, as I told you, have we, yet, the conveniency to Plow much Land, because of the roots and Stumps of Trees; and if we should [54] spend a deal of Time to Root it all out of the Land, which would be very troublesome, we should also, thereby, spoil a great part of Land, by digging for the Roots, and casting the deep barren Sand on the Face of the good Land; yet I own we may, very advantageously, take the trouble of digging the Land with Mattocks, Hoes, or otherways, and Sow *English* Grain thereon: Wheat and Pease in *December*, Oats the beginning of *January*, and Barl[e]y in *February*, all which I have found, by Experience, will be Ripe, and fit for Harvest, to be Housed the latter end of *May*, or a week in *June* at farthest; and then, forthwith, put in *Indian* Corn and Pease, from which I have found, by experience, it may produce as good a second Crop, the same Summer, as what was planted early in the Spring of the Year; which second Crop will be ripe in *November*; which said Husbandry, if it would once become common in the Country, would much encourage the Production of *English* Grain, which I would willingly do my utmost Endeavour to promote.

[55] S. Question. *Is the Making of Tar and Pitch very advantageous to the Country Planters that can, conveniently, otherwise employ their Family of Slaves or Servants in Planting of Corn and Rice?*

J. Freeman. To those that has Plenty of that Wood of which it is made, they find it very profitable, and would give great Wages to hire *Negroe-men* for the Purpose, if they could be procur'd at Hire.

S. Question. *What; is Servants and Slaves so scarce as not to be hir'd for the Country Planter['Js Conveniency to manage their Plantations to the best Advantage?*

J. Freeman. 'Tis very rare that any Freeman will hire himself to Labour, after his Term of Four Years are expir'd, by reason they can employ themselves very advantageously in their own Business, and on their own Land, by Planting of Corn and Rice, as aforesaid; and 'tis also very seldom that any Man will hire out his Slaves to others, but will employ them in following Plantation Business for himself, their Labour being [56] well paid for in their Crops: Or otherwise if they make Tar and Pitch; the

Planter needing not fear to get Sale for his Goods, for Merchants Shipping from *England*, and elsewhere, is seldom wanting at *Charles* Town to carry off the Commodities of the Country, which generally sells at very good Prices for the Planters['] Gain and Advantage.

S. Question.   *But how shall a Man, when first free of his Time, employ himself on his own Land, unless he hire himself a considerable Time at Yearly Wages, or otherwise, to get Money to purchase Land, Implements of Husbandry, and some Stock to begin withal?*

J. Freeman.   When a Servant hath serv'd his time, he may, on Request to the proper Officer, have land assign'd him from the Lords Proprietors as an Encouragement to People to resort thither,[10] only paying a small Yearly Rent, and then, if he is an industrious labouring Man, he may be credited by the Town's Merchants, or Shop-keepers, for necessary Implements for his present Use, and like[57]wise with his Neighbours for a little Stock to begin withal, and then by his Care and Industry in few Years, especially if his Hogs thrive well, he'll be able to enlarge his Stock of Cattle, and purchase more Land, and also, by Degrees, purchase Slaves to work with him in his Plantation.

S. Question.   *What Price may a Man purchase a Slave for at the best Hand? And what Sorts of Money is current for Payment, and what Value is it in Proportion to Money here in* England?

J. Freeman.   An *Indian* Man or Woman may cost 18 or 20 Pound, but a good *Negro* is worth more than twice that Sum, we have passing as currant amongst us the *Spanish* Money, Pieces of differing Value according to its Weight, the smallest Money that we have is call'd Half a Ryal, in Value with us Three-pence Three Farthings, then a whole Ryall Seven-pence half-penny, and double Ryall Fifteen-pence, all which passes by Tale, so doth *Dutch* Dollars at Five Shillings, and Half Dollars at Two Shillings and Six-pence; but [58] all other, except Mill'd Money, goes by Weight, either Silver or gold; the *English* Crown is there worth Seven Shillings and Six-pence, and other Money, whether Silver or gold, by Weight or Tale, is valued at near the Same Proportion in all our Payments; we have also, of late, stamp'd Bills of Credit on the Publick, payable and current as Money from Hand to Hand, these Bills are of several Values, and at last, payable out of the Publick Treasury of the Country.

S. Question.   *I see it hazardous for a Man to give so much Money for a Slave, and that Slave may soon die, then all his Money is lost.*

J. Freeman.   Is it not so here If a Man purchase Cattle or Horses, how can he be assur'd of their Lives? Yet we have a greater Encouragement to buy Slaves, for with good Management and Success, a Man's Slave will, by his Labour, pay for his first Cost in about four Years at most, besides his Maintenance, so, the Remainder of his Life, you have his Labour as free Gain, we esteem their Eating and Wearing as little, for that rises on [59] the Plantation, and is little cost out of Pocket. When they are imploy'd chiefly on planting Rice, and it proves well, a Slave[']s Year[']s Work may be worth the Master 25 or 30 Pounds. There is some in the country, that makes 1000 or 1500 Pounds a Year of the Crops of Rice that their Slaves doth plant, hoe, and manage for them as aforesaid.

S. Question.   *Suppose a Man and his Wife come free into the Country by Paying for their Passage, and have not wherewithal left, or are not willing or desirous to enter forthwith on a Plantation of their own, and in Business of that Nature for themselves, what Methods would be proper, or may such take after they come there, before they are better able to settle for themselves?*

J. Freeman.   Such may hire themselves to some planter, to be Overseer over the Slaves, and take care to Command, and Direct them in their Work without in the field, and the Woman to manage within, for which they may have 25 to 30 *l. per Ann[um]* Wages, if not more, if well capable of that Employment; or, otherwise, they may agree [60] (as is frequently done) with some planter to Live on some other Plantation of his, not what himself

Lives on, for it's very common for Men to keep several plantations at once in their own Hands to manage: Then, when such agreement is made for two or three Years whereon they sometimes have a Slave or two to help them in their Management, with whatever Stock the Owner hath on the Plantation: The Owner allowing him, or them, to Order Business thereon to their best Discretion for Profit; out of which Profit, for their Care and Management of the Business, they usually have, according to the quantity of the *stock* thereon, one fourth, sixth, or eighth part of all the Calves that are Yearly fallen, which Bred up, and divided at about a Year Old, but continu'd to Grase on the same Land till their Time is expir'd; and one half of the Increase, or Profit from the Hogs, or Swine, and one half of the Corn, Pease, and Rice, they can sell from off the Plantation, and half of the Profit, if any arise, from the Dairy, Fowls, and the like, besides what they have occasion to spend, or [61] use in the Family; all which, in a few Years, enables a careful Man and his Wife to settle well on a Plantation of their own, with Stock and Crop rais'd by them on another Man's Plantation, which many have done at their first beginning, and are now masters and Owners of Plantations, Stock, & Slaves, on which they Live very plentifully, without being oblig'd to Labour themselves, as most Jusment-renters are here, or Men of small Estates; neither are Men necessitated to straighten themselves often, with providing, Quarterly, or oftener, to pay great Taxes, Rates[,] Rents, and Assessments as here, which takes from an *Industrious Man* the Profit of his own laborious Care and Industry.

S. Question. *If you have not great Rents, and Taxes, to provide, yet I suppose your Planters are rated to support the Necessities of the Poor, and to repair your Churches, and other Occasions the Parish requires to be assess'd on them.*

J. Freeman. As we have not yet, any common Publick Taxes on the Province, so we have no occasion to be rated to the Maintenance of Poor, neither is there any such Thing, all [62] People that are Free may forthwith imploy themselves so Advantageously to their own Benefit, for themselves, or under some other Planter, that they need not any such supply for their

Occasions. I never yet saw, there, any man, Woman, or Child, in the Country, beg an Alms; neither do I know any Family so Poor and in Want but that, if a small Gift of any kind of Provision was offer'd them, because 'twas suppos'd they could not subsist without such Helps, they would refuse it, and scorn the Acceptance thereof; for I truly affirm, That a Laborious and Industrious Man, being settled for himself, may, with his own Labour and Industry, maintain a Wife and Ten children, sufficient with *Corn, Pease, Rice, Flesh, Fish, and Fowl*, without such Assistance from Others['] Charity.

S. Question. *What Sorts of wild Beasts have you, that is serviceable to Eat when a Man hath kill'd them?*

J. Freeman. Bears, Young or Old, if Fat, is much esteem'd by many Men, that the Flesh is almost comparable to Hog's or Swine's Flesh; Deer's Flesh is the same as here, but not so much esteem'd, because so common that few Planters, especially in the Out settlements, is not long without some in their Houses; for *Deer* is very plentiful in the Woods; and men are not hinder'd, as here, from killing them, or any other wild Creatures. We have store of *Rabbets*, which, in shape and bigness, are [63] much like the *Hares* in *England*, but not in colour; and *Squirrels* also, which are very good Meat. *Rackoon[']s* Flesh, tho' smaller than *Mutton*, hath much the same Taste, and is commonly kill'd with Dogs, which is a good Recreation: But *Wolves, Tygers, Foxes, Alligators*, and *Possumes*, are not Eaten, unless by Native *Indians*, who often use them at their Pleasure, to Eat as other Flesh.

S. Question. *What Creatures are those* Allegators *and* Possumes *you mention?*

J. Freeman. *Allegators* are Creatures living sometimes on the Land, but mostly on the Water in Summer time, but in the *Winter* they sleep in Holes on the *Land*; they have four short Legs, a flat Head, and long Nose; the Fore-part like a Beast, but hard Scales, under the Fore-Legs, and at the Navel lies a little Bag of Strong Musk, from the Hinder-Legs backward, like a Fish; when they Walk, their Bellies trail in the Ground; they are, if full grown, as big as a large *Swine,* or *Calf,* and will destroy *Hogs* and *Calves* on the Land, or at a River-side, when they come to Drink, by seizing and drawing them into the Water, and then sink down with them, till their Prey is Drowned. The *Possume* is a Grey Creature, somewhat bigger than a Cat, that, after they bring forth their Young, six or eight at a Time, they again receive them into a false Belly, they can open and shut at their Pleasure, like a Pouch, or Purse, in which the Young stick fast to the Tets, or [64] Dugs, within the said Belly, sucking them whilst the Dam carries them therein, to seek her own Food.

S. Question. *Are none of these Creatures dangerous for Men whose Business requires them to walk often in the woods?*

J. Freeman. These and all other wild Beasts that I know, will avoid People at Sight, tho', doubtless, if assaulted, and could not otherwise find way to escape, or avoid a Man, Nature would instruct them in self Defence. The most dangerous Creature that I know of, is the *Rattle-Snake;* they, if trod[d]en on, unseen, in the Grass, or otherwise, will Bite that which Offends them; after which, if there is not proper Means us'd forthwith, the poisonous Venome flies up-into the Body, and is Mortal; but there is a certain and infallible Cure for it, which many People carry in their Pockets in Summer time, whilst the Snakes are Abroad, out of their Holes, for they Sleep in the *Winter,* which Medicine is call'd *Snake-Root,* being Chewed and some lay'd to the Wound, and more swallow'd, doth soon expel the Poyson.

S. Question. *Your Land being generally level, have you therein any small running Streams of Water, Rivolets, or Rivers; and what sorts of fish do they produce?*

J. Freeman. Some running Streams we have, tho' not so frequent as here, that rises from your craggy mountainous High-land, and Torrently runs down into your Vallies. Where-ever our Streams rises it glides [65] on, gently, till it meets our larger Rivers, of which the Country is well stored; and on the

Rivers, almost every Planter has the Pleasure of Sailing or Rowing with their Slaves, Carrying or Re-Carrying their Goods to or from their Market Town, or otherwise where their Business requires them, in Boats, or, as we call them, Canoes, or Periagoes, kept by the Planters for that Purpose, in which their Carriages is much more pleasant, and less troublesome than Land-Carriage: But as to your Question: I say our Fresh-Water produces *Trouts*, but, Differing from these here; there is Plenty of *Sturgeon*, which is so valuable here in *England* amongst Gentry; then we have *Cat-Fish*, which is a good Dish, and very plentiful; *Mullet, Mud-Fish, Eels,* and many more Sorts I cannot now remember. Then, in the Salt-Water Rivers, we have a differing Kind of *Mullet,* and extraordinary plentiful; in Taking of them there is great Pleasure, when in a dark Night we in our Canoes, go a Fishing in the River, and in two or three hours take great Numbers of them, by Burning Handfulls of the Wood of which the *Tar* is made, and making a Noise, the Fish are therewithal, and by the Light, so startled that they leap in great Numbers out of the Water towards the Light, and many fall into our Canoes[.] I have taken at a time Eight or Ten Dozen, some as big as a Man's Arm, or Hand-Wrist, others less. We have Store of *Bass, Drum, Sheeps-head, Rock, Whitings, Shads, Cod, Plaice, Flounders, Crabs, Turtles, and Oysters* in great Quantities, from the Shells of [66] which we make our Lime, *Muscles, Cockles, Shrimps,* and others I cannot now name: Then there are other Sorts not eaten, such as *Porpoises, Grampoises, Sharks, Dog-Fish, Garb, Stingray, Saw-Fish* and some others: There is a small Sort of Fish somewhat like a *Crab,* which we call *Fiddlers,* comes out on Land, in great Numbers, on which our Hogs feed.

S. Question.   *Have you Plenty of Wild Fowl in the Country, and of what sorts are they, and when seasonable?*

J. Freeman.   We have Plenty of Wild Turkies in our Woods, and continues all the Year, sometimes 40 or 50 together in a Company, they are great Eaters on Pease in the Fields, but often their bodies pays for the Trespass; some say they have kill'd *Turk[e]y-Cocks,* when fat, in the Fall of the year, that have weighed Thirty Pounds, or more, I have kill'd from a Tree, with a single Bullet, a Turk[e]y (weighing Twenty Pounds) whilst looking down on the Dog that Tre[e]'d him, which stood Barking underneath till the Turkey fell. About the Middle or latter End of *November* there comes from the Northern frozen Climate great Numbers of *Brant* and *Grey Wild-Geese*, the latter is the best Sort, but the former most numerous, some Men have kill'd, in a Winter Season, as many *Geess[sic]* whose Feathers fill'd them a good Bed, or more, those who are diligent, often shoot a Dozen, or more, at a Shot amongst the great Numbers of them when Feeding on these Marshes, which they frequent till *February*, and then return. We have, in the Winter, several Sorts of *Wild-Ducks*, and very plentiful, but the [67] *English* Kind is the best, which are usually fat, and they are very common, and not hard to come within Shot of them in Ponds and Creeks where they frequent. We have *Widgeon, Teal, Curlew, Shell-Drakes, Cranes, Pelicans, Gannets, Sea-Larks, Snipes, Wild-Pidgeons, Partridges,* and many more Sorts of small Land-Birds, three very Noted for the Cage, the *Mock-Bird, Red-Bird,* and *Blue-Bird,* and several other Sorts not here in *England.* A man that is a good Gunner and Fisher may find himself and Family with sufficient of Flesh, Fish, and Fowl, that he may very plentifully kill, whilst he is Recreating himself therein. Some Men hire a Native *Indian* for some Cloathing of small Value and supply them with Powder, Shot, and Bullets, for which they'll supply the Family with Store of either Flesh, Fish, or Fowl thro' the Year, the *Indian* reserving to himself the Skins of the wild Beasts that he destroys.

S. Question. *What Sorts of Wild Fruit and Useful Roots do your Woods afford?*

J. Freeman. Besides the *Black Mulberries, Wall-Nuts, Hickory-Nuts, & Chinkapine-Nuts,* which is a Kind of small Chestnut, and six Sorts of *Acrons[sic]*, we have Variety of *Wild Grapes, Plumbs, Medlers, Cedar-Berries, Myrtle-Berries,* of which Wax is made by Boiling them, *Huckle-Berries, Bill-Berries, Wild Potatoes,* which are very serviceable to Hogs, and many more; we have *Sumack, Sasifrax, China-Root,* Two or Three Sorts of *Snake-Root,* and Variety of other Physical Roots, Herbs, and Flowers which pleasantly adorn our Woods when the Season of the Year requires.

[68] S. Question. *You have given a Description and Account of a very plentiful Country for Food, sufficient for the use of Man, and pleasant withall, as well as profitable, but People's Cloathing, I apprehend, is very dear, for which reason I suppose they go meanly Habited in their Apparel, your Country People not having the Conveniency, for Want of Plenty of Wooll, to make Cloth for themselves as many People doth here, for their common Uses both of Woollen and Linnen, which save many the Expence of Buying.*

J. Freeman. It is customary with us for our Planters to use what Quantities of Wooll our small Flocks affords us, but there is a Custom to add to the Wooll, in Weaving, one Half of Cotten, which every Planter may have grown plentifully of his own, of which a very good Sort of Cloth for common Use is made, and serviceable; likewise, from the finest Cotten the good Huswife spins and makes Cloth for many Uses instead of Linnen. It were to be wish'd that we had Store of People that knew well how to manage Hemp and Flax, which I have found will thrive well, thereby to lessen the Price of Linnen; yet, altho' *English* Linnen and Woollen is much dearer there than here, considering that People, the greatest Part of the Year, goes very thin clad, and airy, and not Wearing out Half the Cloathing there as here, for which Reason they can well afford to buy good Cloathing, but especially fine Linnen, which most common People frequently wear; that, and the Buying Implements of Husbandry for the Plantation, and Hous[e]hold Goods, are [69] the greatest Occasion the Planters have to expend their Money, seeing few or none have seldom Occasion to buy Provisions of any Kind; and they may also order their Affairs so, as to have several Kinds of good Liquors which may arise off their own Plantations, if they carefully provide for it, yet I own, most Men are so bewitch'd or delighted with the beloved strong *Rum,* (*Rumbullion* or *Kill-Devil,* as a certain Author calls it) that they think no Liquor comparable thereto, yet many People, especially Women, rather use, *Made[i]ra* Wine.

S. Question. *Then, certainly, good Husband-men and good Huswifes may (if they are careful and industrious) have any reasonable Necessaries from their own Industry, and may live very plentiful, and thrive in the World, and become Rich, since there is few Occasions for the*

Planter to expend his Profits that arises from his Labour and Industry, which we cannot do here, since Rents, Rates, Taxes, and several other constant Payments requires us to lay out what our greatest Care, Labour and Industry can provide from Time to Time, therefore I think it would be prudent in many of us to remove and take up our Habitations there, and live plentiful and at Ease, especially those whose Substance is small, and cannot live here without hard Labour and Toyl; neither will that suffice them to provide Necessaries for their Necessities, but above all it would be much to the Advantage of poor Labourers to remove thither, whose hard Labour cannot, by their Daily Wages, provide Food sufficient for their Families to support themselves without Want, unless assisted by Allowance from their Parish, or some other Charitable Means, [70] which, in these very expensive Times for Taxes, Men of small Estates, or Jusment-Renters, cannot well afford to [give to] the Poor, and not feel the Want thereof themselves: But what think you; would laborious, industrious, and provident Tradesmen benefit themselves, and live well on their Trades, if they came there? Or what Handicrafts Tradesmen do you find wanting in the Country that would be Beneficial to themselves if they came there to exercise their several Occupations?

J. Freeman. Such Trades as these would be very welcome in the Country, and would much benefit themselves by going thither, their work or Wages, being much dearer there than here, that is to say, a *Bricklayer*, and Maker, *House-Carpenter*, *Mill-Carpenter*, *Ship-Carpenter*, *Sawyer*, *Joyner*, *Wheeler*, *Gun-Smith*, *Black-Smith*, but especially a good *Edge Tool-Maker*, *Weaver*, *Cloth-Dresser*, *Taylor*, *Tanner*, *Currier*, *Shooemaker*, *Sadler*, *Hatter*, *Glover*, *Potter*, and many more that I cannot now remember: Women that are good *Huswifes*, good *Dairy-Women*, *Knitsters*, *Semstresses*, *Spinsters of Wollen*, *Cotten*, *Hemp*, and *Flax*; and either Men or Women that can manage it well from the Seed, to the *Spinner*, would be very serviceable to themselves therein.

S. Q[uestion]. *My Friend, I fear I have tir'd you in Answering me so many Questions, and yet I have more to ask to the same Purpose, but, first, pray accept of a* West Country Farmer's *Dinner, a good Piece of Fat Beef, and Plumb-Pudding, with some other Necessaries, to which,* *and our Country Liquors, you are heartily welcome, and afterwards I will again desire a Continuance of our Discourse on this Subject.*

J. Freeman. I freely accept your Offer.

The End of the First Part

The Second Part
of the
DIALOGUE
Between
James Freeman, *and* Simon Question.

Wherein is very Advantageous Proposals for the Settlement *of People in General, in* South-Carolina *but Particularly for the Benefit of the Laborious Poor. Proposing:* First, *How they may be Settled in a Plantation of Fifty Acres of Good Land, with Stock, and other Necessaries, thereon, as their Own, altho' they have not Money to Buy.* Secondly, *How an Industrious Man and his Wife may, with One Hundred Pounds, Settle himself, to his great Advantage, in a Plantation, worth them Yearly, by their Industry, Fifty* Pounds per Ann[um]. *And* Thirdly, *How, with One Thousand Pounds, a Gentleman may Settle himself on a Plantation worth him, at least, Four Hundred Pounds* per Annum, *whereon they may Live Pleasant and Plentiful.*

J. Freeman. Master *Question,* Now we have Eaten, and Drank plentifully at a Good Dinner, let us return to our [72] former Subject of Discourse; Therefore now propose what other Questions you yet desire to be Resolved in.

S. Question. *Pray what is the cost, or price of a Passanger[']s passage from hence to* Carolina; *and from what Ports doth Shipping frequent that Country?*

J. Freeman. From *Bristol, Biddiford, Exetor,* or *Topsham,* and *Leverpool,* the usual price is five or six Pounds payable here, for Passage, and Victualling thither, for Men or Women, and half Price for Children; but if pay'd there, is at least half as much more:

From *London* many Ships goes thither, but Passage thence is commonly seven Pounds, pay'd down before the Passenger enters on Board. There is many other Ports in *England, Scotland,* and *Ireland,* from whence Shipping Yearly resort thither.

S. Question. *There is many Thousand of poor Husbandmen and Labourers, with their Families, and Tradesmen with their Families, that might well be spar'd hence [here] where they cannot well support themselves without the Assistance of their Parishes, or otherwise: But these cannot pay their Passage thither; neither do I apprehend such will be accepted as Servants for Four Years to pay for their passage over?*

J. Freeman. It cannot be expected that any Man will pay Passage for Children that are uncapable to Work for their Maintenance, but it were heartily to be wish'd, in Behalf of such poor families that would be desirous to Transport themselves thither, that the several Parishes to which they belong would encourage and assist them with Supplies to pay [73] their Passage, or such of them as are so Young that cannot be entertain'd as Servants for Four Years; by which Means the Parish may be discharg'd of future standing Expences, which, in short Time, might equal the Cost of their Passage, and they thereby attain to considerable Substance, and prevail with some others of their Relations to follow them at their Charge, which has been observ'd already from some: But there may also another Way be propos'd to those that are pleas'd to promote the Interest of the Poor that might be dispos'd to Transport themselves. Which is this; That the Parish, or any Friend, or Friends, would lend them, tho' never so poor here, as much Money as would carry them thither, and take their Obligations to repay it again, with Interest, in Four or Five Years, by Causing it to be return'd in Goods to Merchants of the Port from whence they took Passage. For in that Time, if Life continues, they will, very probably, be capable to repay it, and have a Foundation of Substance left them, whereby to live well, and get Wealth: And tho' it may be alledged, if such were so intrusted; yet when at that Distance, if they were not Honestly Inclin'd to repay it, there could be no Means us'd, by their Creditors here, to oblige them thereto, in that Country. In Answer to which, I say, If such should then prove Dishonest, and not be inclinable to pay their just Debts, after three Years from their Arrival, for so long the Laws of the Country doth Protect them, in order to enable Debtors to make themselves capable to pay [74] their Debts: I say, after three Years any Debtor may as well be Sued, and Obliged to pay there as here; nay better, for no Debtors are permitted again to go off the Country, till their Creditors are satisfy'd; and any Creditor may, from the said Sea-port, or otherwise, find some fit Person going thither, to authorize to Sue for, and recover full Cost and Debt, on such dishonest Men, if they prove so; so that whoever would be so Friendly, to support a poor man with the Lent of so much Money for that purpose, which they would be safely Re-paid (unless Death prevent it) would therein befriend them more, than if he had the Gift thereof, and to continue here in Scarcity, Poverty, and Want.

S. Question. *Truly, my Friend, these Propositions seems very Reasonable, and would also be Profitable to many, if Parishes that are much burthened with Poor, that are able to Work, and nevertheless, cannot Support themselves thereby, such Parishes, I say, if they would approve thereof, and be therein assistant to such poor, they would much advance the Interest of the Parish in general, in Time, by useing such Means to lessen their growing Parish Charge; and also greatly advance these poor People, to the means of gaining Riches to themselves, and encouraging others to follow the same Methods?*

J. Freeman. If the Parish Officers, and principal Pay-masters, would consider well their future Advantage, they might encourage, Yearly, a few of their poor People to Transport themselves thither, on the aforesaid Conditions of being Re-paid again, whereby their Parishes, now much Burthen'd, would, in few [75] Years, find themselves very easie Charged, and have their Money, first Lent to the Poor, well Re-pay'd with Interest, and Blessings for such great kindnesses Charitably design'd towards them, whereby they would soon be enabled to provide a very good Maintainance for themselves, and Families hereafter, which would be a very good Christian Charitable Deed to the Poor, and, in few Years, would become very Profitable to themselves thereby, in easeing, and much lessening their

Burthen, in paying constantly to the Relief of such poor People, had they continued in their Parishes.

S. Question. *This seems to me very Reasonable, and in the Main, not Chargeable; yet it requires a good Stock to pay for one Familie[']s removal, especially such that have many Children; which seems to me, they should not be able to Re-pay again, for so many, in so few years, as you have Propos'd.*

J. **Freeman.** If so, some of the Children may be placed out as Parish Apprentices, as is customary amongst you, and in few Years, the parents (as I have known) would freely encourage, and be at the Charge to bring their Children after them, tho' they went thither so poor themselves; by which Parishes would soon find the Benefit.

S. Question. *Truly, on deliberate Consideration, I shall endeavour to further and promote, by my Advice, and otherways, what in me lies, hereby to Advance the Benefit and Advantage of the Labourious and Industrious Poor of my Parish, that are, nevertheless in want of Assistance, which I am satisfy'd, will be a very Charitable act towards them: And also, in my Judgment, it would be Pro[76]fitable for many other Men, that have small Substance in the World, that they would freely remove thither, by which Means they might, by your Description, soon encrease their Substance to Admiration.*

J. **Freeman.** What I have Inform'd you, is nothing but real Truth, and in several Particulars, I am very short of giving that Country its deserv'd Commendation: If you Read a little Book, Intituled, *The* English *Empire in* America[11] and another, Intituled, *A Letter from* South Carolina, *by a* Swiss *Gentleman;*[12] in either of which Books you will find a greater Commendation, and Description, in several things, which I omit, and have not given you an Account of. The Authors of these Books, deservedly, compares[sic] *South-Carolina* to the most Pleasant Fruitful Countries of the known World, *viz. Canaan; Smyrna; China; Japan; Barbary; Persia; Syria; Egypt; Aleppo;* and *Antioch:* And I find that those who have experienced the Country, do allow that it exceeds their former Expectations before they came thither; yet I acknowledge that extravagant, careless, and bad Husbands may, in few Years, destroy their Substance, Health, and Life also, if negligent of its Preservation; tho' it is generally esteem'd that Climate prolongs Life to temperate people somewhat stricken in Years when they come thither.

S. Question. *If there could be a Means prescrib'd whereby the poor Parents of Children could go over, and have their Passage pay'd for them there, probably their Parishes would supply them [77] with the Gift, or Lent of Money, to pay for some of their Children's Passage with them, that the Parents may have, and take, the present Care of their own Children?*

J. Freeman. I can make Propositions something to that Effect, which I think may be well worth Acceptance from any industrious poor Man and his Wife, either Tradesmen or Husbandmen, but especially Young married Couples, who may, by the increase of many Children, be reduc'd in few Years to as great Necessities as many others before them. To such, I say, as are desirous to go thither to advance themselves, if they can use no possible Means to pay their Passage over, which discourages them, as then not being in Circumstances proper to enter themselves as Servants, being married, and having Children, or likely to have some within the said Four Years; yet I say to give all possible, needful, and necessary Encouragement to promote the Benefit of such Men and Women as are, and will be carefully laborious, industrious, and honest in their Undertakings, and are desirous to remove themselves thither for their Advantage; which I am heartily desirous to promote for the future Benefit of any of my honest well-meaning, tho' poorest, Country People, for whose Sakes I have receiv'd Instructions from a particular Friend and Acquaintance of mine, Living in the Southern Part of *South-Carolina*, which, in my Judgment, is the pleasantest and most plentiful part of the Country, who have purchas'd, from the *Lords Proprietors* of the *Pro*[78]*vince* several Thousand Acres of good Land in that Part of the Country, which Land lies yet uninhabited, and no Improvements thereon, nor Benefit or Advantage receiv'd therefrom, only by Pasturing it with Stock of

Cattle. This Gentleman, I say, having authoriz'd me to make very advantageous Proposals to any good Husbandmen and their Wives, or Tradesmen, which must consequently be of great Advantage to them that will accept thereof, and are not of Ability otherways to get Passage thither.

S. Question. *I shall gladly bear these Advantageous Offers in their Behalfs, therefore pray proceed in a Rehearsal of the Particulars?*

J. Freeman. The said Gentleman is willing and free, partly for the Reasons aforesaid, by his Agent here in *England,* to agree with honest poor Men to these following Articles:

N.B. That such good, laborious, honest Husbandmen, Tradesmen, good Huswifes, or labouring Women, whether single Persons or married, that will go thither as Servants for Four Years, as aforesaid, to receive, during the Time, such necessary Wages as shall be needful for them to provide necessary Clothing during the Time of their Service; or otherwise to have such sufficient Necessaries provided for them, to which Purpose they shall be Friendly treated and agreed with by the said Agent, and Passage provided for them the first Conveniency, after such Agreement is so made, and when arriv'd there [79] shall be kindly receiv'd into the said Gentleman's Service, and courteously dealt withal during the said Term, provided the said Servants prove faithful and honest in their Undertakings; and at the Expiration of the same, the said Servants, if married or single, shall forthwith receive these farther Encouragements from their said Master; the Particulars whereof to be contracted for, and agreed to, before the said Servants['] Departure from *England,* which are as follows:

Imprimis. That the Gentleman, by his Order or Appointment (immediately after the expiration of the Servant[']s said Term of 4 Years) cause Fifty Acres of his Land, good and fit for Corn, Rice, and Pasture, to be Measured out as a Plantation, for the said Servant. On which Land so Measur'd, and the Timber thereon growing, the said Gentleman to grant, forthwith, a Lease to the said Servant, his Executors, Administrators, and Assigns, for a Term of any certain Number of Years, not exceeding Nin[e]ty Nine, nor less than Thirty One, or otherwise for three Lives, without payment of any Fine for the Same.

Item. The Gentleman then to assist his Tenant with Materials, and Labour, in building a House for his present necessary Occasions, without Re-payment for the same.

Item. That the Landlord supply his Tenant with some necessary Hous[e]hold-Goods, and Implements of Husbandry, for the Plantation Use, for which the Tenant to pay at Two Years end.

Item. That the landlord furnish his Tenant [80] at his enterance on the said Plantation, with Three good *Cows* and *Calves;* Three young *Ewes* and *Ram;* One *Farrowing Sow;* and one Couple of the several kinds of Tame Fowl usually kept on Plantations; whereby the Tenant will, in few Years, attain to good Stock, for which he [is] to pay, in Kind, or Value, at Two Years end.

Item. That the Tenant is also supply'd with a sufficient quantity of Corn, Pease, and Rice, and good Beef or Pork; and other Necessaries for their present spending, till their Crop comes in; and Seed-Grain, of all sorts, necessary; for which the Tenant to pay, in Kind or in Value, after the first Crop.

Item. The Tenant to pay only Five Shillings in Sterling Money Yearly, during the Term: And, in order to promote good Husbandry and Huswifry, they to pay Yearly, in Kind, a small quantity of the several Kinds of production the Plantation would afford by Industry, the particulars to be mentioned in the Agreement (and in Value, about Five Pounds Sterling Money) and to arise from the Plantation, whereby their Rent will very easily be discharged. And also to clear from Trees and Shrubs, and Enclose and Fence in, Two Acres of land at least Yearly, till Forty Five acres, of the said Fifty, are Cleng'd; and not above Seven or Eight Acres to be in One Field: All which Conditions will tend to the Tenant's particular Advantage. And these several Propositions being very Advantageous in behalf of such as are of no Substance, wherewithal to carry them thither, [81] would in my Judgment, be very sufficient inducements, to such poor People, to encline them to desire to Transport themselves thither on such Conditions.

S. Question. *It's true, these Propositions are very inducesive, and probably will be gladly accepted by such Single or Married Persons,* *having no Children with them, nor likely to have any: Yet this has but little reference to induce those who have, or may have Children to be provided for, during the Term of their Service.*

J. Freeman. To such Poor, who having Children to bring with them, if they are above Twelve Years old, and their Parents consent thereto, their Passage also may be paid, and they entertain'd and provided for by the said Gentleman, as Apprentices, till they arrive to the Age of One and Twenty Years, to be employ'd in necessary Business on his Plantation, or in some Handicrafts Trade; and at their attaining the Age aforesaid, Then to enter on a Plantation of Fifty Acers[sic], on the several conditions aforesaid. But in case the Children are younger, it would be proper that they were bound out as Apprentices here in *England*, before the Parents depart hence, or if not, if they can procure some Means, whereby to pay the Passage of such Children, either of themselves, or by the assistance of their Friends or Parishes: Such Children may also be receiv'd and entertain'd, on the said Gentleman's Plantation, during the time of their Parents['] Service; for which the Parent to enter into an Obligation to pay the said Gentleman, within Four Years after Freedom from [82] their Service, the Sum of Three Pounds Yearly, for the Maintenance of every such Child, during the Time; and the like Sum for Children Born during the time for their Service, if any; which is but a very small Consideration for their Maintenance, and Learning in the mean time, and a considerable Time given, or allow'd, for payment thereof. In order to prevent Objections that might arrise, to Discourage honest poor Men and their Wives from Transporting themselves, on the aforesaid Conditions, who having Children that cannot otherways be provided for, or dispos'd of, must have some such-like Ways, or Means, propos'd, or else their designs of going must be obstructed. It is not reasonable to be expected, that one Man should take on him the burthen of paying Passage, and Maintenance, for such Children as are no ways capable of Service.

S. Question. *Suppose a Family, or single Person, having sufficient to pay Passage over, and not wherewith[al] left beside to settle them in a Plantation, may such, without entering as Servants, be receiv'd* by the said Gentleman, on the aforesaid Conditions, as his Tenants, for the said Term, if they desire it, or is it limited only to such as serve their four Years?

J. Freeman. These Propositions being Designedly to promote and encourage People's resorting thither, for their Benefit and Advantage, it therefore, seemingly, were unjust, if any that pays their Passage, and thereby going over Freemen, should be excluded, or deny'd the Priviledge of becoming Tenants on the aforesaid Conditions, if they desire it, provided they [83] propose, and make such Agreements with the Gentleman's Agent here, before their going thither; which if done, they may be assured of being forthwith, after their arrival there, receiv'd as Tenants on the said Conditions.

S. Question. *Truly, I take these Propositions to be extraordinary generous in the Behalf of the Poor, and as I ever took you for my real Friend that would relate to me no more than the real Truth, So, you will herein much befriend such Poor as shall be desirous to Transport themselves on such Conditions, if you and the said Gentleman take such Methods, that these Generous Proposals may be effectually performed, to such honest People as are desirous to accept the same. My good Friend, These Profitable and Welcome Propositions, in behalf of good honest laborious People, deserve their hearty Thanks, and Prayers for the good Success of the Undertaker. Come, here's to you a full Glass, it's that Gentleman's Health; your Friend in Carolina; wishing him, and all others that are so Generously Inclin'd, for the Publick Good of other Men, as well as their own Private Interest; Good Success in their Undertakings therein.*

J. Freeman. I'll Pledge you freely a double Glass; wishing, That many Parishes would freely contribute, and encourage poor People to go thither, not only for the Poor[']s Profit, but their own Ease hereafter.

S. Question. *Is there any of our West-Country-Men there Settl'd, that proves good Husbands, as well, as good Topers of your Strong Liquor, which is so frequently Drank there?*

J. Freeman. We have many, of late Years, from *Wiltshire, Dorset, Sommerset, Gloucester,* and [84] *Devonshire,* and some from most Counties in *England* and *Wales;* some proves good Husbands, too many bad, which loves Strong Liquor to Excess, so well, that they prefer it before Wealth, Health, nay, Life itself, as have evidently appear'd of late, in many *West-Country-Men* coming there, which tended to their discredit in the eyes of sensible, sober, and temperate Men; for we may certainly conclude, that such Abusers of themselves, by Intemperance, cannot be esteem'd as Sensible Men, that will destroy Wealth, Health, and Life with all, for the Enjoyment of a momentary Sottish, intemporate, Life and Conversation.

S. Question. *As you have made very Advantageous Proposals, in behalf of the Poor; which is heartily to be wish'd, were, or might be, put in prosecution, by many Parishes; Can you also prescribe any profitable Propositions, if a Gentleman of good worth should be inclinable to go thither?*

J. Freeman. If a Gentleman of good Substance, and of a generous Spirit, to promote Others['] good besides his Own, he might much advance (in my Judgment) his Successors, and be benefited himself also thereby, if he apply himself to the Lords *Proprietors,* which, at this time, is the Noble *Henry* Duke of *Beaufort,* as *Palatine;* the Honourable Lord *Cart[e]ret;* Sir *John Colletine; Maurice Ashl[e]y,* Esq; Mr. *John Danson,* Merchant; Lord *Craven,* a Miner; these Living in or near *London,* often at a Board meet and consult publick and private Business, relating to the Province of *Carolina;* there is also one Proprietor living in *South-Carolina,* Mr. *Blake,* a Miner; and one Mr. *Trott,* as a [85] Proprietor, living in some Foreign Plantation.[13] Now, I say, if a Gentleman applying himself to the Board of Proprietors, may, on very reasonable Terms, purchase a large Tract of Land, and procure many poor Families to go with him to Inhabit the said Land, which, in time, will be Profitable to him or his Successors, and by carrying with him a considerable Quantity of *English* Goods, may therewith purchase Slaves and Stock, build a good House, and reap the great Profit thereof, by planting and otherways, as I have before describ'd, and Live on the same as

Noble and Splendid as above six Times the Value thereof, lying in an Estate in *England,* could here Maintain him in: I say he may there reap the Profit, Pleasure, Honour, and Satisfaction, that a Blissful, Retir'd Country Life can afford Mankind, he not being there hurried in Multiplicity of Publick Affairs to molest or disturb his quiet innocent Pleasure, and plentifully enjoy the Fruits of his Diligence, and Delight, in Improvements on a large and pleasant Plantation, adorn'd to his greatest Satisfaction, with Buildings, Fish-Ponds, Park, Warren, Gardens, Orchards, or whatever else best delights him not being liable to a continual Burthen of Payments to the Publick, for whatever he possesses, but that there he may enjoy himself, Family, Neighbours, and Friends, with all the innocent, delightful Satisfaction imaginable.

S. Question. *Suppose a Man comes thither, who hath about One Hundred Pounds Stock to bring with him in* English *Goods for Sale, and design to sell the same and settle himself on a [86] Plantation, what may that purchase for him in Order to live well, and to what Value may it return to him Yearly, and keep the principal Stock, still whole and entire in Value, or Increasing for the Benefit of his Successors? Pray, how would you advise such to begin?*

J. Freeman. I will, to the best of my Judgment, acquaint you therewith: *N.B.* We'll suppose if a Man hath 100 *l.* and no more left, only some Hous[e]hold Goods, after the Passage of himself and Family is pay'd here; In the first Place I would advise him to apply himself, by Letter, or otherwise, to the Gentleman that is *Secretary* to the *Lords Proprietors,* his Name, and Place of Aboad, may be known at the Carolina *Coffee-House in* Birchin-Lane, *near the* Royal-Exchange, London, from whom (after the Money is pay'd for the purchase of one or 200 Acres of land, or what other Quantity a man desires to buy) he will then receive an Order to have that Quantity of Land survey'd, or measur'd out for him after his Arrival, in any such Place as is not already taken up, or possess'd, by some other Person; and after he hath the Land survey'd or measur'd, by the proper Officer appointed there, the Officer then returning into the Office for that Purpose, a Map, Plot, or Plan of the Land, how and where, it is butted and bounded, with Land-Marks according as it lies, and the Place where, then forthwith the Purchaser hath from the said Office a *Purchase-Deed*, Sign'd and Seal'd, Intitling him and his Heirs to that Land, under Payment of a small Yearly Acknowledg[e]ment to the *Proprietors* as chief Lords in Fee for ever.

[87] **S. Question.** *What will the Purchase, and other Expences therein, amount unto for 100 Acres of land so bought from the Proprietors?*

J. Freeman. As I told you before, the Land is purchas'd at so very easie Terms from the *Lords Proprietors*, to encourage Men thereto, that whosoever intends to purchase and settle there, will not be discourag'd by an extravagant Price, seeing the Price of 100 Acres there will not amount to as much as Ten here, as I told you at the Beginning of our Discourse. When a Man resolves to buy, the certain Price will be at first demanded by the said *Secretary*, without Delays in Bargaining, as is here between Seller and Buyer, so that 'tis not material to be inform'd therein till a Man fully resolves to purchase.

S. Question. *May not a Man purchase Land there in the Country, after his Arrival, when he hath seen and chosen the Place he best likes?*

J. Freeman. He may if he please; but if it proves to be Land already taken up by some other Person, he must then buy it from him, at several Times the Value of the first Purchase; but if it is not taken up by another Man, then the Purchase-Money is to be remitted thence to *England* to the *Lords Proprietors*, as by a late Order by them made, and the purchaser shall then have the Land granted him in Manner aforesaid.

S. Question. *What will you advise next to be done by such a Man with the Remainder of his Hundred Pounds, at first propos'd?*

J. Freeman. That he buy and carry with him from *England* several Falling Axes which [88] is narrow, thick, and strong; Hoes, Wedges, Maul-Rings, Saws, and other Tools or Implements, proportionable to his Working-Family he intends to employ, and Nails of several Sorts, and other Irons necessary for Building his intended House, and a Steel-Mill of the best Sort us'd here to grind Malt, but there to grind *Indian* Corn for his Family's Use; or if he buys greater Quantities of either than what he expects may serve his own Use, it will there sell to good Advantage. And the Remainder of his Money, laid out in Goods, such as before I mention'd as is usually carry'd from hence thither, which, if bought here to the best Advantage, will there yield him double the Price it first cost here, by which his Hundred Pounds will purchase him 150 Acres of Land, and Necessaries to build a House for present Use, and Tools, or Implements for the Plantation Use, and Goods for Sale sufficient to yield him there 150 Pounds, which he may again disburse, or lay out to settle himself well to his Advantage; Thus, supposing him to arrive there in *September, October,* or *November,*

l.

Imprimis: {Two Slaves; a good *Negro* Man	45
{And a good *Indian* Woman	18
Item, Expences in Splitting Clapboards, Sawing Boards, Side-Posts, Rafters, Shingles for Covering, and Workman's Wages in Setting it together, besides his own Labour	10
Item, Expences for Eating and Drinking, Eight or Ten Months; for Five or Six in Family, till his *Harvest,* or other Eatables comes in Kind	20
Item, A Canoe, or small Periogoe to carry Goods in	4
Item, Two Farrowing Sows with Pigs	2
Item, Six Ewes and a Ram	5
Item, Sixteen good Cows and Calves, and a Bull	30
[89] *Item,* For several Necessaries belonging to a good Huswife for the Dairy Use, and Poultry of several Kinds to breed from	6
Item, Remaining in Hand for other extraordinary Uses that Occasion may require before Money may return from the *Plantation*	10
In the whole	150

All which arises from the Remainder of his 100 *l.* the first Stock in hand, with which, by the Calculation, or Computation, which is as near as I can compute it to the Value; a Man has 150 Acres of Land for a Plantation; an indifferent good Dwelling-House for present Use, Slaves to begin to labour with him for Profit, and the Settling Conveniencies on his New *Plantation;* a good Breeding Stock thereon; Necessaries for the good Huswife in her Dairy; and Cows sufficient to give Milk to make Profit from the same; Provisions for the Family till more arise from the Plantation, and Money still left in Pocket to defray other extraordinary Expences that Occasions might require, so that a careful diligent Man, and a good Huswife, is at once settled with this 100 *l.* in a Prospect of Reaping forthwith by careful Industry, great, good, and profitable Returns; the Man and his Negro, being well employ'd by Planting; the good Huswife and *Indian* Woman, diligently Employing themselves, in the careful Management of the Dairy, Hogs, and other Profits that might arise from her Diligence, by which they will reap delightful, and profitable Returns with their Industry, and their Stock of Goods, and Slaves encreasing, and live more plentiful, get much more Money, and be at less extraordinary Expences than if they enjoy'd in *England* 30 *l.* Yearly Estate [90] of their own Inheritance, I cannot say Freehold, seeing all Estates are here liable to so many Taxes, Rates, Assessments, and other Disbursements, which takes away one Half, if not two Thirds, of the Value, by which Time the Owner has but a small Yearly Income remaining for himself, and his Family's Use, tho', at the same Time, if his Estate is valued at 30 *l. per Annum,* and in fee-simple, he esteems it worth at least Six Hundred Pounds, and yet cannot raise scarce enough from it, besides Disbursements, to maintain himself and a small Family handsomely thereon: Whereas you plainly find, by this Computation, One Hundred Pounds *Sterling,* well manag'd in a Plantation in *Carolina,* affords far greater Profit than Six Times as much here: I'll now suppose the Profits to be much less, than may well be rais'd on the said Plantation; *As thus,* The Planter and his *Negro* Slave to Clear, Fence, Inclose, Plant, Hoe, Harvest, and Thrash only four Acres of *Rice* for Sale, besides *Corn, Pease,* and other Things I mention'd before, as necessary on the Plantation for the Family's Use, and for the Stock of Hogs or Swine, which Four

Acres is probably worth, if a tolerable good Crop, and at a moderate Price, not less than Eight Pound *per* Acre, when fit to sell to the Merchants, besides small broken *Rice* for the Family.

S. Question. *Excuse me, Mr.* Freeman, *for Interrupting you; I have ask'd you several Questions relating to your Husbandry, but omitted, or forgot to inquire, in what manner your Rice Grew in the Stalk and Ear: Pray, before you proceed further, resolve me therein?*

[91] *J. Freeman.* The manner of its being Planted in the Field, I have already acquainted you: *After which, as it grows up, there shoots out many Branches, or Stalks, from one Root; when grown to its full Height, [it] is as tall as good* Wheat *here, but the Ear shoots forth and the Grain hangs thereon, much like to the Oats here in* England, *which it nearest resembles to any* English *Grain that I can compare it unto:* But now to proceed. The profit from the Dairy we cannot reckon less than Twenty Shillings Yearly, from each Cow, if any care is taken therein; and seeing Butter and Cheese sells there so well, it may well be reckoned at double, nay treble that Sum; but I will account it, as before, at the least Profit from the Dairy, and say only Sixteen Pounds the first Year; which added to the Thirty Two Pounds for *Rice*, makes Forty Eight Pounds for that Year's Profit; then what additional Profit may probably arise the following Years, by the Increase of the Stock, and Profit from Pork and Beef, your self may judge, and at the same Time consider, that tho' I have now computed, that the Planter had bought only 150 Acres of Land, yet his Stock is not at all restrain'd from Feeding on Six Times that Quantity of Land, seeing there is little Inclosures, & no Notice taken of Trespass in Eating Grass that is there plentiful, much more than the Cattle can generally destroy; (it being customary, in the Month of *March*, to burn, as it stands, great Quantities of the dry Russet Grass) so that you may hereby very apparently see a great Disproportion in the Profits of a small Estate here in this Kingdom [92] and what the Value thereof, if manag'd there, would amount unto, which would much advance such Men for their own present Benefit, and continue still Increasing by Care, for the great Advantage of their Successors.

S. Question. *Truly, by this Computation which you have now made, it seems extraordinary profitable for such as will go thither, and become good industrious People, may in few Years arrive to great Substance, if he can but lay a Foundation of 100 l. and if not, Labour and Industry in Time (I find by your Description) will gain it. But again, suppose I, or some other Country-Farmer, Gentleman, or any Man that is inclinable to go thither, and become a Gentleman Planter, who will not work himself, but can raise 1000 l. Stock to buy Goods here, and carry thither for Sale, and if he likes the Country, resolves then to purchase Land, and settle himself thereon, with the aforesaid 1000 l. worth of Goods when sold, to be again laid out in all Necessaries proportionable thereunto, how will you propose, it may best be done? And what Yearly Profits may probably arise from thence by a moderate Computation, and keep the main Stock whole and entire, or rather Increasing for Posterity?*

J. Freeman. If you, or any Friend designing so to do, that could raise such a Sum of Money, after Passage is pay'd for himself and Family, and as many good Servants, as he can conveniently procure, I would then advise, That he purchase, before his Departure, 1000 or 1500, Acres of Land at least, and receive the Proprietors['] Warrant to take it where he shall desire the same, after his Arrival there; then to furnish himself with Hous[e]hold-Goods, [93] Implements for Plantation Use, as aforesaid, and Necessaries for Building a House for present Occasions, which may afterwards be employ'd as a Kitchen, when, by the Profits from the Plantation, he has built a fine Brick-House thereon, so that after these Conveniencies are discharg'd, the Remainder of the 1000 *l.* to be laid out in proper Goods as aforesaid, for to be sold in the Country, (which according to the aforesaid Proportion of 100 *l.* when so lay'd out) there will amount from the same about 1500 *l.* which may thus be dispos'd of again to settle him in a Plantation, worth him at least 400 *l. per Annum,* at a very moderate Computation, Accounting the Money thus lay'd out;

1.

Imprimis; Fifteen good *Negro* Men at 45 *l.* each.........	675
Item, Fifteen *Indian* Women to work in the Field, at 18 *l.* each, comes to	270
Item, Three *Indian* Women as Cooks for the Slaves, and other Hous[e]hold-Business.......................	55
Item, Three *Negro* Women at 37 *l.* each, to be employ'd either for the Dairy, to attend the Hogs, Washing, or any other Employment they may be set about in the Family	111
Item, Thirty Cows and Calves at 1 *l.* 15 *s.* each, and Two Bulls at 1 *l.* 5 *s.* each	55
Item, Two Mares and one Stallion at	40
Item, Six Sows and One Boar, ...	4
Item, A large *Periogoe,* and *Canoe,*	20
Item, Twenty Ewes, and a Ram, ...	14
Item, Four Oxen for a Cart, ...	10
Item, The Cart, Chains, Yokes, and Conveniencies,..	10
Item, The Charge to Carpenters for a small Boarded-House for present Use about	20
Item, For 500 Bushels of *Corn, Pease,* and *Rice,* unshell'd, for the Slaves for the first Year, ...	62
Item, For Twenty Barrels of Beef,..........................	25
[94] *Item,* For Five Barrels of Pork, ...	15
Item, For to buy several Necessaries for the Dairy, and Fowls of several Sorts for to kill, and also to breed from, ...	10
Item, For Wine, Rum, and Sugar for his own Drinking at Home,...	10
Remaining in Hand for other extraordinary Uses that Occasion may require before the year comes round to receive *Profits*	94
	1500

The whole being 1500 *1.* suppos'd to be Receiv'd for the Goods brought from *England.* Now, for a moderate Computation what these Slaves may bring their Master, Yearly, to be employ'd in Planting, *viz.* The fifteen *Negro* Men, and Fifteen *Indian* Women, I'll suppose they Clear, Fence, Plant, Hoe, Reap, &c. only Three Acres each, which is but Nin[e]ty in the whole, Thirty Acrers [*sic*] of that in Corn, Pease, Potatoes, Pompions, and other Things, to be made use of in the Family, and amongst the Hogs: The other Sixty Acers, to be Planted with *Rice* for Sale; from off which, we'll suppose, each Acre affords a Thousand weight, as is usually observ'd, fit for the Merchants, besides what is broken and kept for Family Use, and that Sold at but 15 *s.* the Hundred which is cheaper than usually it is Sold there, that amounts to *Seven Pounds Ten Shillings* the Acre: So that the whole Sixty Acres comes to 450 *l.* for One Year[']s Crop of Rice; but if it prove a very good Crop, and Sells at *Twenty Shillings* a Hundred, as it doth often times, then the profit is much more; therefore, within compass, I may safely compute that after the Slaves['] Clothing is discharg'd, which, at most, [95] is not *Thirty Shillings* Yearly to each, there will Remain 400 *l.* Profit, besides what is made from the Dairy, Beef, or Pork, or any other way, and the Slaves and Stock Yearly encreasing: Also, after the first Year, the Field-Labouring Slaves, will Plant and Manage more Acres Yearly, than what I now Computed. So, by this you find, a Man having here in *England,* an Estate of Inheritance to the Value of 1000 *l.* which is but 50 *l.* Yearly Value; and that not to be reckon'd half his own, seeing he must pay, at least, the other half away to other Uses; but if that Value was here laid out, as aforesaid, in Goods, wherewith to Settle in *Carolina,* he may, thereby, make it worth him there, as perpetual, 400 *l. per Annum,* That is, provided God blesses his endeavours, and gives Health and Life to his Slaves, till the Young ones grow up, as the Old decay. Now is not this sufficient inducement to Men of Substance, to carry it thither, and settle themselves so much to their advantage, as this doth evidently make appear?

S. Question. *This, now, so well pleases my Inclinations, I find my Ambition begins to desire, that I were a Man that could raise a Thousand Pounds, to make my self a Man of 400 l. a Year therewith. I tell you, my Friend, I will, at leasure, compute what I can raise, by selling all my Substance, that is my Lease-Hold Estate of 60 l. a Year, and all my Stock and Crop, with some Money lying in store, will come up* *to near that Sum. I assure you, if my Wife will comply therewith, I'll endeavour to be your Neighbour once more,* Here, [96] Maid, bring us a Bottle of the Best. *Come, my Friend* Freeman, *here's to you heartily; to our good Neighbourhood once again. Now will I set up for a Man of* Four Hundred a Year, *wherewith I'll Breed and Maintain my Family with Credit and Honour.*

J. Freeman. Master *Question,* I'll as heartily pledge you, again, and again: And do seriously advise you, or any other Friend, whether Rich or Poor, That they will weigh Matters, and really desire, and resolve to use their utmost Lawful Endeavours, to advance and prefer themselves to a more plentiful and profitable Way to Live, than now they can propose to do, in this Kingdom, according to the usual Examples I now see, unless it is Gentlemen of great Estates, or great Userers, whose Moneys are not so heavily Tax'd.

S. Question. *I remember you told me of several sorts of Tradesmen, that would be very profitable to themselves, were they there; but then, I suppose, they must settle in some noted Town of Trade, in order to profit themselves thereby?*

J. Freeman. Any of them Trades, which I mention'd to you, may find Business enough to employ themselves in, and much to their Advantage, if they settle in the Country, on Plantations, by that means they'll be free from the Daily cost and expence, which a Family requires, in the Town, for House-Rents, Provision, Firing, and other Necessaries, that must all be bought there, whereas, in the Country Plantation, it arises from off their own Land, without that Daily Charge; and the Tradesman follow[s] his Employ, also, in [97] the mean time, whilst his Family's maintenance, and other profits, arises from off his Plantation.

S. Question. *There are other sorts of Tradesmen, whose Business requires them to live in a Town; such as Merchants, Mercers, or Shopkeepers, as we call 'em here, and other Trades you have not Named. Would such find good Business, Profit, and Encouragement, in any of your Towns?*

J. Freeman. Yes, doubtless, were such dispos'd to come thither with a quantity of Goods, and Settle in *Charles-Town,* they would find (as others there have, and still do) great Profit thereby, and grow very Rich, in few Years, as many there have done, from a small Beginning: But if any Friends or Acquaintance of mine, who were enclinable to follow such Business, and go thither with a Stock of Goods, for the Planters['], or *Indians[']* Uses, I would heartily recommend, or advise them, to Settle themselves at a considerable distance to the Southward of *Charles-Town;* which is, as yet, all the Towns of Trade, that Ship[p]ing doth resort unto: I say, if such Merchants, Shopkeepers, and other Trades, were Settled about 80 Miles to the Southward of *Charles-Town,* at a certain Place call'd PORT ROYAL, where has been and still is intended, another good *Sea-Port Town* to be settled, for a conveniency of Trade for the Inhabitants.[14] Such Merchants, or Tradesmen coming thither, with good Stocks of Goods, as aforesaid to furnish the Inhabitants, and *Indian* Traders, with such Necessaries as they want, would soon grow extreamly Rich, as many of the [98] Merchants, Shopkeepers, and others did, at the first settling their Trade in that Town, and doth still so continue getting Riches, to Admiration, many of them being now worth many *Thousand Pounds,* from a very small Beginning.

S. Question. *Is this Place, call'd* Port Royal, *likely to be a good Port for Shipping to Trade unto with Safety, and without greater Danger than is at* Charles-Town? *And is it probable, that a Town in that Place would attain to a good Trade, to vend their Goods of all sorts, as* Charles-Town *Merchants and Shopkeepers now do?*

J. Freeman. Without doubt: In time it will become a Place of great Trade, there is no probability to the contrary, it lying at that distance from *Charles-Town,* all the Inhabitants in that part of the Country, will gladly repair thither to be supply'd with Goods. It also lies in the Trading-way to many Nations of *Indians* that *Charles-Town* now supplies with Goods. At which Place, if those that Trade amongst the *Indians,* could furnish themselves with Goods for that purpose, and sell their own, they would gladly spare the trouble of going thither. If there was at that Place, in

Merchants['] Custody, sufficient of all sorts of such *English* and *West India* Goods, as the Country requires, especially *Indian-Trading* Goods, as we call it, There might certainly be sold Thirty or Forty Thousand Pounds Worth of Goods Yearly, at this Time; and much more were there a Town well settled, provided they buy the Country Commodities again for Exportation. It were heartily to be wish'd, [99] and I know Hundreds that are Masters of Families, and *Indian* Traders, would joyn with me to encourage Merchants by Enjoyning our selves constantly to buy and sell, for a certain time, on reasonable Terms, with such Merchant, or Merchants, that should there first settle a standing Stock, or Store, of all Necessaries to furnish People withal, and also to purchase the Country Commodities, whereby they may be continually supply'd: And this I am well assur'd of, if any Gentlemen, Merchants, or others, would in Partnership joyn and lay out 10 or 12000 *l.* in Stock of Goods which would be sufficient at present to carry on such Business, by or with, their Factors there, as might clearly get them (with good Success at Sea) at least 5 or 6000 *l.* on their Returns.

Were I a Man that could raise such a Stock for that Purpose, and settle on that Place, I question not in the least of getting 5000 *l.* a Year there clear, provided (as aforesaid) Shipping was successful at Sea.

Or were I worthy to be entrusted with such a Stock, I would gladly content my self with the Overplus (as my Profit) after I had Yearly accounted to have deliver'd double the Value there, in Commodities, to what I receiv'd in prime Cost.

But to return to your Question: As to the Safety of the Place for Shipping to resort unto, it is generally adjudg'd by those that knows well the River, that it exceeds for (Safety and Depth of Water, for large Ships,) the River that leads to *Charles-Town,* and they may very safely come up to the Place where the Town [100] is design'd, and 300 Acres of Land reserv'd from being sold by the *Proprietors* for that Purpose.

S. Question. *But I should think you have not People enough yet to the Southward of* Charles-Town *to create such a Trade with Merchants, if they were there at* Port-Royal *to take off 30 or 40000 l. Worth of Goods Yearly untill you are become more Populous.*

J. Freeman.   I own we our selves (that is the *English* Subjects) are not numerous enough there to expend so much Goods; but the great Trade that such Merchants would forthwith contract with the *Indian* Traders that Trades amongst many Nations of *Indians,* which would soon take off so much Goods, which is now carry'd from *Charles-Town* that Way, to the Value of many Thousand Pounds more Yearly, there being many of that Business that Trades that Way, the least deals to the Value of 500 *l.* a Year, some to the Value of One, Two, Three, or Four Thousand Pounds Yearly, in such Goods as the *Indians* use.

S. Question.   *By the Description you have given me, I apprehend, and am well satisfy'd therewith (the Truth thereof I make no Doubt, but really conclude) that* South-Carolina, *and especially the Southern Part thereof, is a very good Country for People that go from hence thither, either Rich or Poor, Merchants, Tradesmen, Gentlemen, Husbandmen, Farmers, Labourers, Men or Women Servants, Boys, Girls, and Children, wherein they may live Healthful, Pleasant, Plentiful, and get Riches withal to Admiration, provided they live temperate; but to those that lead intemperate Lives,* [101] *delighting themselves in Drinking to Excess of your Strong Liquors,* Rum, Punch *and* Wine *doth, of Necessity, so inflame their Blood, in the hot Summer Months, that it cannot otherwise be expected than to create Feavers, or other violent Distempers, that proves Mortal especially to People at their first Coming, and Change of Climate, before they are somewhat naturalized thereunto.*

J. Freeman.   As I have told you before, I say truly, I have not exceeded, to my Knowledge, the Truth in any Particular; and this is observ'd that People Coming thither from any part of the *English's* Dominions, are so well satisfy'd therewith, that not One of a Hundred desires again to leave the Country, and return back from whence they came.

CAROLINA is esteem'd, at this Time, the most profitable *Colony,* or *Plantation,* that *America,* or any other Part of the World, affords, especially for the Husbandmen or Planter; *Therefore* were my Advice acceptable, or worthy of being taken Notice of, which I would freely, heartily, and cordially, and without Deceit, give my honest Country-Men and Women, of what Quality, Ability, or

Degree, soever they are, if capable of any of the Business I have before prescrib'd as proper to be us'd there, I would advise many Thousands of all Sorts aforesaid, that they would repair thither, and that the Rich, as well as the Poor, would freely go thither with their Substance; and as it is natural that he who hath sufficient desires and endeavours for more, so there it may be found by Industrious Care; and to those who have here sufficient, and will be [102] therewith content, without going farther to improve their own Interest and Advantage; To such, I say, I heartily wish, desire, and advise them to Encourage, Advise, and Assist others of their Acquaintance, especially the honest and laborious Poor, and they, therein, will do themselves good Service in Decreasing, or Preventing a Parish Charge, and also extraordinarily befriend such Poor, whom they shall so advise, and assist in Removing thither, which most Parishes might well do for their Poor's Advantage, by Raising a Joynt Stock of Money, in Order thereunto, to be Yearly employ'd to that Use, whereby they will find their standing Charge lessen'd, or prevented, and no Doubt, will reap farther Advantages for being so Christianly charitable to their Poor, whether it be by them given or lent; if the latter, the aforesaid Gentleman, if they become his Tenants, and live Five Years, he will undertake to secure and return the Money for them, back to *England* in Goods, to some Merchant to pay the same justly to the said Parish, or People, by whom it was lent.

S. Question.　*But suppose many Families that pay for their own Passage, should resolve to go together in company in Ships, and come there unexpectedly into the Country, would they not then be reduc'd to Necessities, for want of Provisions, and other Necessaries, till they are Settled, and have had Time to provide it, of their own?*

J. Freeman.　As I acquainted you before, if any Passengers come Free, by paying their own Passage, if they have not wherewithal left them, to Settle themselves to their liking, [103] and buy Provisions, and other Necessaries for themselves, till their Plantations produce it them, such, I told you, if they agree here in *England*, with the Gentleman's Agent, before they go thither, they may, forthwith, be provided for, by the said Gentleman, or by his Order, as his Tenants, soon after their

Arrival, as aforesaid; and to such as go thither well provided in Substance, need not fear buying Provisions, or other Necessaries they want, till they are well Settled, to have it rise from their Industry. Yet, if a considerable Number of People, as *Free-Passengers*, should form a Design, and Resolution, of going thither together, in one Ship, or more, or near the same Time, designedly to Settle there in a Neighbourhood with each other, it would be proper that they sent a trusty Agent before them, or to some proper Person there in the Country, to chuse convenient Lands for them, and purchase Corn, Rice, and other Provisions for them, at the best hand, to be ready, at their Arrival, for their use.

Or if such Company would, a Year, or more, before their going thither, Collect, or make a Joint Stock amongst themselves, to send and settle a Plantation, in common amongst them; with Slaves, Stock, and House to receive them at their Arrival; and to entertain them till they could conveniently seperate themselves, and enter on their several Plantations: This would be a good conveniency again to receive their Friends hereafter, at their Landing, and to support their Sick, or Poor, if any such come with them, till they are capable to provide for themselves.

[104] Tho' this Country doth not abound with those gay and noisie Amusements, as great Towns and Cities here affords, to affect and please the Rich, and such as delight therein, and cannot Recreate or Content themselves without it. Yet, for such as have experienced the Frowns of Fortune, and will lay hold of this Conveniency, and affect a Country Solitude, Contemplation, Planting, Gardening, Orchards, Groves, Woods, Fishing, Fowling, Hunting Wild Beasts, and many other innocent Delights, which are frequently there; And those who with a small, or no Fortune or Substance here, would desire to provide some competent fixed Settlement, for themselves and their Children, there cannot be found a Place in the *British* Dominions, that will better answer their Expectations: For a Man may there begin, and yet live comfortably, with as little Substance as in any Place whatever, and, perhaps, with less, as, I think, I have evidently shew'd you. Now the properest Time for Passengers to remove thither, is to procure Passage from hence, at such time that they may, probably, be there between *August* and *December*, for two Reasons; That is for Health sake; for then they have

several Months of Cool Weather; and the Heat comes on them gradually. And also for Profit sake; that being the properest Time to begin a Settlement, as before I describ'd to you.

S. Question. *But if many People, in great Numbers, especially the Labourious sort, should find Means to remove thither, would it not be Objected against, as detrimental to the publick good of the Crown and Kingdom?*

[105] *J. Freeman.* That appears to me very improbable, for 'tis very apparent, I think, that most *Cities, Towns,* and *Parishes,* in this Kingdom of *Great-Britain* and *Ireland,* have more poor labouring People than they can well employ; whereas, were the Overplus of good Labourers settled there, it would be a Yearly Advantage to the *Crown of England;* for most Commodities brought from thence hither, pays considerable Duty here, especially *Rice,* which pays Four Shillings every Hundred Weight; so that if every Labourer plants only Two Acres of *Rice* Yearly, that is brought over to *England,* tho' afterwards Transported off again to other Countries, that Two Acres being computed not less than a *Tun* Weight, which is of considerable Value, whereby every such Labouring Man profits the *Crown of England* Four Pounds Yearly, which will be of great Advantage.

S. Question. *I am now satisfy'd as to that, but I foresee that many Poor Ignorant People that would be inclinable to go thither, will alledge many Doubts and Scruples, against going to Sea, of which many People have, I think, a causeless dread on themselves; that is, such Doubts as these.* I am willing, and desirous to go thither, but the Sea-Sickness will kill me, or some of my Family; we cannot endure that Sickness. Then the danger of an Enemy; If we should be taken, we are undone during Life; Or otherways, the Ship may Founder in the Sea, and we all be Drownded: Or if we should have a cross ill-temper'd Commander in the Ship, he'll not, perhaps, allow us half Provision enough to live on till we come thither; *or some other* [106] *such like scrupulous Fancies will discourage them, so that they'll chuse rather to live here at Home, and continue Mean, Poor, and Miserable, perhaps in Want, during Life, rather than adventure themselves for Six Weeks or Two Months Time in a good Ship.*

J. Freeman.   No Doubt there is some, thro' Ignorance and Folly, may use such, or the like, weak Reasons to discourage them, but on deliberate Consideration, or Enquiry, they may conclude, and be assur'd, that this *Sea-Sickness*, tho' troublesome to many, yet all are not Sick, and none dies of that Sickness, but are much more the Healthier when these sick *Qualms* are past, or they come on Shore again, besides, it seldom lasts long, perhaps a Day, or Two, or Three, and then as hearty and good Stomachs as ever: And as to the Danger of the Enemies, which I hope God will prevent, by Giving us a *Lasting Peace*, but if *War*[15] should continue, and they should have the Misfortune of being taken, which doth not often happen to Ships that goes with good Company, or Convoy, then such Ships and Cargo is generally bought again at that Time from the Enemy, and then the Ship proceeds on in her Voyage with the Passengers; or at worst, if they are made Prisoners, it is but for some Time, and they are then freed again; and then if the Passengers hath ensur'd their Goods to the Value, they are repay'd their Loss again by the Ensurers: As to the Fear of the Ship's Found'ring in the Sea, or by some other Accident they may be drowned; if they go out in a good Ship, they may as well fear [107] or distrust the Falling of their House on their Heads when the Wind blows, for the same Almighty *Providence* protects People *on Sea as on Land*. And as to the last dangerous Consideration of Filling a hungry Belly; if there is any such Cause of Distrust, Agreement may be first made with the Ship's Owner, or Commander, and Obligations thereunto; that the Passengers shall have, during the Voyage, a full Proportion of Victuals Daily deliver'd them, as the Sailors themselves have, and that they have *Beef*, or *Pork*; and *Pudding*, or *Pease* therewith; at least Three or Four Days a Week, which with Five or Six Pound of *Bisquet-Bread* a Week, deliver'd to each Passenger, and other Sorts of Victuals the other Three or Four Days, and *Beer* and *Water* sufficient, *then if they come on Board as lean as* Pharaoh's *poor Cattle, they may be like fatted Porks at their Arrival*, unless Winds are so fortunate that the Voyage is made in a Month or Five Weeks Time, as it is often known to be; so that, on Consideration of the full Matter, any sensible Persons will not suffer such weak silly Fancies to prevail with them, so much to fear the Fatigue of one Passage, so as thereby to loose the

Opportunity of what they have in View of Benefiting themselves, during the Remainder of their Life, of which, if they will not accept, they, in Probability, are never like to be in a Capacity of otherwise Advancing their Fortune from their present State and Condition they are now in, to any higher Degree of Riches, Content, or Repute. Now, Master *Question*, pray let us drink a Glass or two of [108] your *Stout October Beer*, and then conclude our Discourse at this Time, for Business calls me hence, this Afternoon, to discourse with some that are fully resolv'd to remove thither for Advancement of their Fortune.

S. Question. *Mr.* Freeman, *here's a hearty Bumper to you, with thanks for this trouble I have given you, in Resolving me these several Questions, by which I find, That People, in general, removing thither, of what Rank soever, either Poor or Rich, they may much Advantage themselves thereby; therefore I shall, and will, not only Resolve, as soon as conveniently I can, to dispose of my Effects here, and remove thither: For these most advantagious Computations you made, for a Man to settle himself, in an assurance (that is, by God's Permission) of at least 400 l. a Year, with 1000 l. prime Cost, hath made such impression in my Thoughts, that I shall think the Time tedious till I arrive in* Carolina, *and renew a good Neighbourhood between us. The same Reasons, methinks, should induce others, that can raise about 100 l. to go thither to Settle themselves, to so great an Advantage; Likewise for Tradesman to resort thither, much to their Advantage; but especially poor Husbandmen, Women, Boys, or Girls, that might so much Advantage themselves, by that Gentleman's generous Proposals to them. But pray,* Mr. Freeman, *let me also know who is this Gentleman's Agent here, for I shall diligently endeavour to prevail with many honest and labourious poor People, to accept of these Propositions you have made them, in the Gentleman['[s behalf: Therefore, pray let me know his Name, and Place of Aboad, that I may acquaint such poor People therewith, as are desirous to Treat and Agree* [109] *with him, on the Articles you propos'd, so that they may make application to him, in Discourse, or Writing, in order to effect, and come to a certain agreement on the premises, and to receive directions from what Port, and when Passage may be gotten; and when certain and positive Agreements are effectually made; that they may have conveniencies of Passage provided for them, and receive particular directions, where they may apply themselves (when* *arrived) to the said Gentleman, in order to have the said Articles and Agreements speedily put in execution, after their Arrival; and that they may be well informed, in what other Things is material and necessary to be, by them, discours'd of, agreed to, or known by them, before their departure out of their Native Country.*

J. Freeman. The Knowledge of the Agent's Name,[16] and Place of Abode, I shall, for some particular Reasons, at this time omit: But at our next meeting, if you acquaint me of any such People that are resolv'd to accept of these Advantageous Proposals, and go thither to have them accomplish'd, I shall then acquaint you, where you, or they, may come to the Knowledge of his Name and Place of Abode, to make such Agreements as aforesaid.

S. Question. *I heartily return your Thanks for you Obliging me with this Description according to my Desire, in doing whereof you are now probably tired with this long Discourse; otherwise, if Time and Business would have permitted your Stay with me longer, I should have desired to have given you farther Trouble to describe to me the* Nations, Natures, Customs, Government, Religions, Wars, Traffick, Apparel, Languages, [110] *and whatever else you know relating to these Native free* Indian *People, which you have often mention'd, and with whom the* English *in* Carrolina, *have Correspondence and Trade withal. But since Time will not permit, let us divert ourselves a little, with Moderation, in the refreshing pleasure of drinking a Bottle or two of our* West-Country Ale *and* Cyder, *which I think is better pleasing to me, than your Strong* Rum, Punch, *or other Distill'd Liquors, will be to me, hereafter, at my coming to* Carrolina: *so here's to you, most heartily, in a Glass of delicate* Cyder.

J. Freeman. With all my Heart; I'll now pledge you two or three Glasses, and then take my leave of you, at this Time, till next Opportunity of meeting you again: At which Time, I shall freely oblige you, with a Relation of what I am acquainted withal, in such particulars as you shall desire to know, in relation to the several Nations of *Indian People,* living within my knowledge, or according to the best Information, that I have received from those whose business it is to converse, and live, frequently, amongst them. Master *Question,* here's one Glass more to you, with Thanks for my good Liquor; and so fare you well till next Meeting.

S. Question. *Mr.* Freeman, *pray remember your Promises; and let it not be long before I see you again, to perform them; Farewell.*

F I N I S

ADVERTISEMENT

Whoever is resolv'd to Transport themselves to CAROLINA as Servants, or Tenants, on the Articles and Conditions propos'd in the 78, 79, and 80th Pages, of this Book, to be effectually perform'd by a Gentleman in CAROLINA, after Agreements are first made between them and the said Gentleman's Agent here in *England, This is to inform them,* That resolves thereon, that they may know the Agent's Name, and Place of Aboad, if they apply themselves in Writing to Mr. *Robert How,*[17] from whom they will forthwith, after Receipt thereof, receive Intelligence according to their Desire; the Directions on their Letters to be worded thus: *For Mr.* Robert How, *to be left at Mr.* Nicholas Brabins, Haberdasher of Hats, *in* Talbot-Court *in* Grace-Church-Street, London; *Post Pay'd.* But *Note,* if Postage is not by them pay'd, their Letters will not come to Hand, whereby they will fail of their expected Answer thereto, which Resolution is taken to prevent the Cost of Percentage of Letters from unnecessary Scribblers that proposes no Benefit thereby, but only to satisfy inquisitive Curiosity.

Whoever is encourag'd and resolves to go to CAROLINA as Free Passengers, or Servants, thro' the Encouragement they find contain'd in this Book, this is to desire, that they would, at their Enterance on Board of the Ship they intend to take Passage in, after Enquiry therein is made by some one of them, to give a particular Account, in Writing, directed unto [112] Mr. *Richard Davis*, Book-Binder,[18] in *Bridg[e]water* of the Ship's Name, and Port from whence she sails, with the Number, Names, and Professions of such Free Passengers, or Servants, as go thither on the said Encouragement, in Doing of which they will oblige the Author, who would gladly, after their Arrival there, have Knowledge thereof to return such Gratifications as may be acceptable for so doing.

N.B. *Any Bookseller, or other, may be furnish'd with this Book in Sheets at 25 s. a Quarter of a Hundred; and in Gilt-Forrels, at 15 s. the Dozen, or 31 s. the Quarter, by* Charles Walkden, *Stationer, at the* Bell *in* New-Fish-Street, *near* London-Bridge; *and* Robert Davis, Bookseller, *in* Bridgewater, Sommersetshire; *where is likewise sold a new Book, entitl'd,* Innocence and Friendship abus'd: Or, Poor Robin's *late Visions.*[19] Price 1 *s.*

NOTES

1. This brief foreword seems to have been the work not of the author John Norris but of the bookseller Robert Davis of Bridgewater, County Somerset.

2. Jusment renters or gistment renters were graziers who rented pasture land for their cattle.

3. For detailed biographical information concerning the eight original proprietors see William S. Powell, *The Proprietors of Carolina* (Raleigh, 1963), 12–49.

4. Although the Charter did allow for toleration of religion, it did not provide that only Church of England ministers could be supported by a public allowance authorized by Act of Assembly. Norris may here be referring to the revised Constitutions of 1670 which proclaimed the Church of England to be the "National Religion" of Carolina and empowered the Carolina Assembly to levy taxes for its support. See Mattie Erma Parker and William S. Price, Jr., eds., *Colonial Records of North Carolina* (Raleigh, 1963–), 2d ser., I: *Charters and Constitutions of North Carolina, 1578–1698*, 181.

5. The act governing the church is in Thomas Cooper and David J. McCord, eds., *The Statutes at Large of South Carolina*, 10 vols. (Columbia, 1836–41), II, 282–294.

6. On the legal status of slaves in South Carolina see M. Eugene Sirmans, "The Legal Status of the Slave in South Carolina, 1670–1740," *Journal of Southern History*, XXVIII (1962), 462–73.

7. The law relating to servants may be found in Acts of the General Assembly, March 2-16, 1696, manuscript volume South Carolina Archives (Columbia), p. 28-30.

8. The statute is printed in Cooper and McCord, eds., *Statutes*, II, 23-25, 182–85. A uniform tax was also levied to pay for the expedition against St. Augustine. Ibid., II, 206-212.

9. Ibid., 200-206, 223, 247–48, 280, 295–97.

10. By direction of the proprietors in 1669 each male servant was to receive 100 acres on the expiration of his time. The amount was reduced to 60 acres in 1679 and to 50 acres in 1682. See R. K. Ackerman, "South Carolina Colonial Land Policies," unpublished PhD. diss., University of South Carolina, 1965.

11. The work Norris refers to is R[ichard] B[urton], *The English Empire in America* (London, 1685).

12. Norris here refers to the companion piece published in this volume,

Thomas Nairne, *A Letter from South Carolina* (London, 1710), from which he borrowed or paraphrased several passages.

13. William, third Lord Craven (1700-1739), inherited his father's the second Lord Craven's share in 1711. Nicholas Trott (1663-1740) received the original Edward Hyde share from his father-in-law Thomas Amy in 1700. In 1707 Trott and his wife also inherited the share that originally belonged to Sir William Berkeley. Information concerning the other proprietors mentioned by Norris is to be found in n. 2 of pamphlet 1, Nairne's *A Letter from South Carolina.* Detailed information concerning the proprietors is to be found in Powell, *Proprietors of Carolina.*

14. Port Royal was initially settled in 1684.

15. The War of Spanish Succession.

16. The agent is identified in the concluding advertisment as Mr. Robert How.

17. Robert How may have been related to Job Howe, a prominent South Carolina political leader at this time.

18. Unless the printer misprinted Richard for Robert, "Richard Davis, Book-Binder" was presumably not the same as Robert Davis, bookseller. The fact that both did business in Bridgewater suggests that, if they are indeed two different people, they may have been related and partners in different aspects of the book trade.

19. *Innoncence and Friendship Abus'd: Or, Poor Robin's Late Visions* has not been identified, but it was probably a reissue of *Poor Robin's Vision* (London, 1677), one of several "Poor Robin" books, most of which seem to have been the work of William Winstanley (1628-1698).

Index

Index

Index

Ferguson, Robert, 7, 22
Fish, in S.C., 37–38, 111
Florida, 37, 53, 84; as Spanish colony, 8, 17, 18
Fortifications, in S.C., 18, 53–54, 95
Fowl, wild, in S.C., 41, 111–12
French, S.C. military engagements with, 17
French, as S.C. settlers, 57, 60, 85. *See also* Huguenots
Fruit, in S.C., 39–40, 112

Gardens, in S.C., 99
Generosity, as a characteristic of S.C. settlers, 58
Geography, of S.C., 36–37
Georgia colony, 2
Gloucester, Eng., 125
Government, of S.C., 21–22, 43–51, 94–95
Governorship, of S.C., 45–46, 94
Great Britain, 42, 140; as cultural model for S.C., 18
Guinea: S.C. trade to, 43
Gunsmiths, 114

Habeas Corpus, in S.C., 48
Happiness: individual, as a social goal in S.C., 26–27, 83–84
Harvest: seasons for, in S.C., 25, 39
Health conditions, in S.C., 16, 92, 120, 137
Hill, Wills, Viscount Hillsborough, 1
Hogs, *see* Livestock raising
Hospitality, as a characteristic of S.C. settlers, 21, 58
House of Commons, British, 1, 22
Housing, in S.C., 102
How, J., 76
How, Robert, 145
Huguenots, French, 20, 57, 85; as proportion of S.C. population, 59
Husbandry: modes of, in S.C., 96–99
Hyde, Edward, Earl of Clarendon, 84, 147

Image: negative, of S.C., 8, 16–17
Improvement: as a social goal in S.C., 18; of S.C. as an English province, 58
Independence: as a social condition, 15; as a social goal in S.C., 18, 26–27, 35

India, 37
Indians: in S.C., 84, 85; as a military threat to S.C., 16–17, 27, 53; as proportion of S.C. population, 59; as slaves, 19, 27, 43, 87, 106; culture of, 143–44; military value of, 17–18, 52; trade with, 12–13, 95, 135–37
Indian trade: opportunities in, 12–13, 65, 135–37
Indigo production, in S.C., 43
Industriousness, as a characteristic of S.C. settlers, 58
Inferiority, of S.C. to Britain, 20–21
Ireland, 88, 95, 117, 140; labor in, 14
Irish, as S.C. settlers, 85

Jamaica colony, 6, 7, 8, 43
Japan, 37, 119
John Carter Brown Library, 3
Johnson, Governor Sir Nathaniel, 3
Juries: method of selection, in S.C., 20, 48–49

Kamil, Neil, 2

Labor: conditions of, in S.C., 86–88; cost of free, in S.C., 105; nature of, in S.C., 14–15; amount of, needed to settle a plantation in S.C., 128, 132
Laborers, wages in S.C., 66
Lahore, 37
Land: ease of acquiring, in S.C., 9–12, 102, 107, 127; fertility of, 10; methods of acquiring, in S.C., 60–61; price of, in S.C., 60–61; tenure of, in S.C., 61–62
Landholdings: patterns of, in S.C., 102
Landscape: anglicization of, in S.C., 20
Laws: as the boundaries of power, in S.C., 44; English, in S.C., 22, 47; process of making, in S.C., 47–48
Leatherworkers: need for, in S.C., 114
Leeward Islands, 43
Le Jau, Francis, 6
Liberality, as a characteristic of S.C. settlers, 21, 58
Liberties: civil and religious, in S.C., 44; English liberties in S.C., 22, 44
Ligon, Richard, 2
Liverpool, Eng., 25, 116

Index

Livestock raising, in S.C., 8, 10, 12, 25–26, 41, 90–91, 100–102
Lombardy, 44
London, Eng., 3, 76, 117, 145, 146
Luxuriance, of agriculture in S.C., 7–11, 80–81

Madeira Islands, 43
Madrid, Spain, 8
Maryland colony, 37
Masons: need for, in S.C., 114; wages in S.C., 65
Material promise, of S.C. as attraction for immigrants, 8–27, 80–81, 84–85, 102, 105–6, 107–8, 113–14, 125–26, 131, 133–34, 137–38
Mental capacities, of S.C. free inhabitants, 21, 58
Merchants: as socio-economic category in S.C., 58–59; opportunities for, in S.C., 126–27, 134–37
Methods, for settling a plantation in S.C., 25–26
Military life: misery of, 35–36
Military organization, of S.C., 51–54
Militia system: in S.C., 17, 51–53; as an appropriate institution for a free people, 35–36
Ministers, see Clergymen
Mississippi River, 37
Model, see Cultural Model
Monck, George, Duke of Albemarle, 84
Montgomery, Robert, 6

Nairne, Thomas: biographical details, 3; *A Letter from South Carolina*, 31–73, 119
Naturalization process, in S.C., 57, 59
Naval stores production, in S.C., 10, 25, 40–41, 95–96, 105
New Bern, N.C., 4
New England, 43
New York, 43
Norris, John: biographical details, 3–4; *Profitable Advice for Rich and Poor*, 74–147
North Carolina colony, 4, 36, 84

Occupational structure, of S.C., 58–59
Officers, public: in S.C., 50–51
Opportunity, see Material Promise
Orchards, in S.C., 99–100

Paper Money, in S.C., 54–56, 107
Parliament, of Great Britain, 1, 22, 47
Parliament, of S.C., 45–46, 85, 94
Peas, see Agricultural commodities
Pennsylvania colony, 2, 8, 43
Persia, 37, 67, 119
Physical characteristics, of S.C., 6–7, 36–37, 84–85
Pitch, see Naval stores
Planters, as socio-economic category in S.C., 58–59
Poor: English, as potential source for emigrants to S.C., 80–81, 117–20
Poor relief, in England, 24
Population of S.C.: character, 57–58; composition of, 57–59
Port Royal, S.C., 12, 135, 136
Poultry raising, in S.C., 91
Poverty: in England, 80–81, 118–19; lack of, in S.C., 15–16, 58, 108–9
Presbyterians, 20, 85; as proportion of S.C. population, 59
Private interest: as motive for settlement in S.C., 23–24; relationship of, to public good, 23–24.
Private realm: expansion of, in S.C., 23
Profits, see Rates of Return
Promotional literature, 2–27
Propositions for prospective emigrants, 116, 120–26, 145–46
Proprietors, Lords, of S.C., 9, 45, 71, 84, 120, 125, 127; value of immigration to, 70–71
Providence, R.I., 3
Psychology of colonization, 1–27
Public good: relationship of private interest to, in S.C., 23–24
Public realm: smallness of, in S.C., 10

Quakers, 20, 85; as proportion of S.C. population, 59
Queen Anne's War, 17

Rates of return, for investment in a plantation in S.C., 24–26, 63–65, 129–30, 132–34
Religious buildings, in S.C., 21, 85–86
Religious composition, of S.C. settlers, 85
Religious development, in S.C., 59–60
Religious diversity, of S.C., 20

151

Wages, for laborers, in S.C., 25, 65–66, 105

Wales, 88, 125; labor in, 14

Walkden, Charles, 76, 146

War: risks of, in S.C., 16–17

Wealth: opportunities to obtain, in S.C., 9–27, 66, 68–71. *See also* Material promise

Weavers: needed in S.C., 114; wages in S.C., 65

Welsh, as S.C. settlers, 85

West-Indies, 7; trade with, 95

Wheat, *see* Agricultural commodities.

Wills: method of probating, in S.C., 50

Wiltshire, Eng., 125

Windsor, Eng., 7

Women: as servants in S.C., 88; need for tradeswomen in S.C., 114

Yamasee War, 3

Yields, agricultural, in S.C., 25, 96–98